Faith Matters

First published November 2000

National Library of Australia
Cataloguing-in-Publication data

Watson, Gordon.
Faith matters : theology for church and world : collected essays.

Includes index.
ISBN 0 9586399 4 9.

1. Theology. 2. Christianity. 3. Theology, practical. I.
Pfitzner V . C. (Victor Carl). II. Regan Hilary D., 1959-.
III. Australian Theological Forum. IV. Title.

230

Published by
Australian Theological Forum
P O Box 504
Hindmarsh
SA 5007

Printed by Openbook Publishers, Adelaide, Australia

Table of Contents

Part One
The Trinity—Being and Self-Disclosure

Part Two
The Church, its Marks and Mission

Foreword

In an earlier book, *God and the Creature: The Trinity and Creation in Karl Barth*, Gordon Watson gave Australia a very powerful, but not uncritical, account of Karl Barth's doctrine of the Trinity and the central role to which he restored it in the teaching of the church. In that book Dr Watson gave considerable attention to the all-important methodological issues which Barth had raised in his great *Church Dogmatics*. In this book he gives more attention to the liturgical or doxological issues in the worship, life and mission of the church, with particular reference to the situation in Australia in respect of the ecumenical, social, and ethical questions with which the Uniting Church in Australia is faced in its public life and on-going mission in the modern world.

Faith Matters is a superb and timely book. In it Dr Watson begins with a rigorous discussion of the Being and Self-disclosure of the Trinity from the perspective of the Holy Spirit, and then proceeds to offer a careful account of the distinctive character of Karl Barth's epoch-making interpretation of St Anselm's *Fides Quarens Intellectum* and *Cur Deus Homo*. His purpose is first to clarify Barth's theological method, with particular respect to the procession of the Holy Spirit and the divergence between Eastern and Western churches over it. It is then only after his careful account of these central issues and only under guidance of rigorous theology, that Watson turns to the pressing questions of the nature of the church, its sacramental life, and the nature of its unity and mission.

This represents a very profound and helpful way of discerning the real issues at stake in the Uniting Church and the crucial problems, theological and sacramental, that have to be faced in any basis of union. Moreover, there are also serious issues of an ethical and social nature which other churches must take up and resolve together, among themselves, and in the world in which they live and are called to exercise their mission: by considering them strictly in the light of Christ and in the context of his healing and transforming relation to the created order.

Such a theological orientation and a clear program in the thought and activity of the church *in Christ*, together with the fresh grasp of the compassion of God and the redemptive place of the Incarnation in the cosmos, have retroactive effect in transcending the divergent conceptions of Law and Gospel. It cannot but be fruitful in healing the kind of division between Reformed and Lutheran traditions that have so often and so long hindered the witness of Christians in the world. Moreover the strong theological and evangelical recovery of the primacy of the Holy Trinity in the life and worship of the churches, such as Dr Watson advocates, cannot but bear fruit today in the personalising and healing of moral and social relations.

Thomas F Torrance
Professor (Emeritus) of Christian Doctrine
University of Edinburgh

Acknowledgments

The essays in this volume represents my experience of the church as a parish minister and theological teacher for nearly forty years. I have been fortunate to have lived at a time in which the church has faced many challenges to its theological integrity and mission. I wish to place on record my indebtedness to some of the significant people who have contributed to my formation as a Christian witness.

My parents, Harold Field and Ethel Irene Watson, whose faithfulness and love, now as members of the church triumphant, accompany me to this day as God's continuing gift. My dear wife Joan and sons Stephen and Michael, to whose patience, love and encouragement I owe more than I can tell.

To my colleagues and students in parish and academy who, through discussion and debate have sharpened my perception of the Christian faith, I say thank you.

My theological position may be best described in the context of the present discussions as that of a 'critical realist'. I am deeply indebted to the biblical theology of the hymns of Charles Wesley and the dogmatic tradition of the Reformed churches. This later has come alive for me in the magisterial work of T F Torrance whose teaching and writings over a period of thirty years continue to be an inspiration for pastoral ministry, preaching and theological writing.

I acknowledge with thanks the editors of *The Scottish Journal of Theology* for several articles reprinted here with some editorial amendment:

Vol 30, 'Karl Barth and St Anselm's Theological Program'
Vol 41, 'The *Filioque*—Opportunity for Debate'
Vol 42, 'A Study in St Anselm's Soteriology and Karl
        Barth's Theological Method'

Gordon Watson
Trinity College
Brisbane

Introduction

Academic theology has rarely if ever been on the 'best-seller' list of books in any country. Likewise, while there has been a resurgence of interest in various forms of 'spirituality' with more people undertaking courses in the study of 'religion', Christian theology does not have a prominent place in state-run universities. In the Middle Ages theology was taught at the major European universities alongside the study of law and letters with large number of students attending classes.

Christian theology was and is concerned with a careful consideration of issues of an in-house nature but also with current issues of a social, cultural and scientific nature. Academic theology does have something to say to the church and to the world and, even if not a 'best-seller', does fulfil a prophetic function. Theology performs a dynamic and enlivening function in the church and for the wider world, which it engages and challenges. It is not concerned simply with the repristination of old formulae or treatises, but is carried out within the community of faith as it attempts, in a systematic way, to make sense of life and the world.

Faith Matters is such an exploration. Though this collection of essays is by a Reformed theologian, it is an ecumenical theological endeavour,. For over forty years Gordon Watson has been involved in the life and ministry of his own Church and the churches in Australia as pastor and teacher.

As first chairperson of the Australian Theological Forum, he promoted the theological enterprise in Australia within an ecumenical and interdisciplinary framework. It is fitting that in recognition of his contribution to theology the Forum should publish a collection of his essays and do so with a Lutheran and Roman Catholic theologian as editors. The selection of essays is his own, with the arrangement and editing of the text the work of the editors.

Introduction

The essays in this volume concern matters of faith. Theology, as words about God, or as articulation of the faith by a faith community seeking understanding, is concerned with reflecting on particular contexts and events. In this reflection and articulation of faith it is not any faith which matters. Christian theology needs to concern itself with the Trinitarian faith, with what God has revealed and continues to reveal in our space and time. Such a faith, and such a theology, is centred on the radical involvement of God with the whole of creation, whereby all of the created order is transformed and reconstituted in and through God's action.

This collection deals with prime topics in theology, the Trinity, the church, its sacramental life, Christian ethics and reflections on theological dialogue. Its essays are arranged so as to reflect this sequence.

It is important to highlight a common and significant theological thred which runs throughout all of the essays and which could have been chosen as the title: the ineffable condescension of God. It first appears in the essay on the Holy Spirit, where Watson writes of the 'ineffable and undivided unity of God's essence' (p 12). Following St Basil, he later argues for the 'congruence of the mystery of the Holy Spirit, in relation to the unity of God's triune life, with the mystery of our own redemption . . . ' (p 15).

This theme can also be found in the essay on the *filioque*, where Watson writes on the difference between Eastern and Western interpretations of the Trinity, suggesting a distinction between 'God's ineffable and undivided unity and the economy of salvation in which the hyspostases act in accord for the purpose of the renewal of the creature' (p 81). In the West, he suggests, theology has had a tendency to modalism and in Eastern Orthodox theology has tended toward subordinationism and tritheism.

In one of the final essays, referring to ethical questions, Watson makes reference to the economic and the immanent Trinity, which he writes 'presupposes an ineffable condescension of God. This condescension of God has, as its purpose, not the revelation of a metaphysical mystery concerning the being of God's inner life, but the creation and recreation of the creature in relationship to God. The economy of salvation takes place not for the enrichment of God's being but for the sake of the creature, that it may participate as a creature in the glory of God's own life and love' (p 152).

While the study of the 'ineffable undivided unity of God's essence' and its implications for the economy of salvation, or an exploration of the divisions between the East and the West on this topic, will never make a 'best-seller' list, they are crucial, if not 'foundational', issues for theology. It is our hope and desire that the book will be read widely and acknowledged as a significant contribution to the theological world.

Victor C Pfitzner
Hilary D Regan
Adelaide
November 2000

Part One

The Trinity: Being and Self-Disclosure

The Holy Spirit: Worship and the Mystery of the Trinity

This paper does not attempt, in F Schleiermacher's terms, 'an explanation in due theoretic form'[1] of the place of the Holy Spirit in the being and life of the triune God. It does, however, attempt to take into account in discussing the mystery of the person of the Holy Spirit the implications of the fact that such discussion is concretely situated in the context of the worship of the Christian community, in the acknowledged presence of the triune God. Such acknowledgment is important, for it opens up the question of the logic, the coherent structure of such statements that may be made about God the Holy Spirit.

The place of the Holy Spirit in theology and church, in the respective ecclesiologies of the Eastern and Western traditions of Christianity, may be understood in an important sense as deriving from their views of the relationship between theology and worship. To appreciate this we begin by making a few remarks about Christian worship in the context of its development in the life of the church.

Christ did not establish a society for the observance of worship, a cultic society, but a church understood to be the reality of a new creation in him. For many, however, the church's liturgy signifies answers to questions such as how worship is to be carried out according to certain rules, together with symbolic explanation of ceremonies. In this context the liturgy is judged according to how it satisfies felt religious or social needs. Paradoxically, the church and, in particular, the individual church member have become the object of worship; it is celebrated for their sake, for their religious nourishment. The liturgy, transformed in this way into a cult, is no longer

---

1. F Schleiermacher, *The Christian Faith*, transl of *Die Christliche Glaube* (Edinburgh: T&T Clark, 1928), par 50.

3

understood as the means by which the church celebrates its creation.

The liturgy of the church and its theology and mission have suffered a fatal divorce. The church as the sphere of God's work in the new creation in Christ, orientated toward the world as the gift and offer of new life, is in many respects understood and experienced as entailing a departure out of the world for the sake of individual sanctification. The origin of this hiatus between the church's liturgy, its theology and mission, is illustrated by the transformation of the church's liturgy into a cult designed for the fulfilment of the individual religious needs of the believer. This does not begin simply with the Enlightenment's bifurcation of reality into the theoretical and practical concerns of reason and experience, a development only emphasised by postmodernism. These developments only underscore basic influences at work in the church from earlier times.

As distinct from the many mystery religions which flourished in the environment of the early church, the church did not proclaim its worship as the object of its faith. It was not a cult in which the worshippers were initiated into higher secrets. Christianity was proclaimed as saving faith, not as a saving cult. The worship of Christianity was not an object of faith. It had no place in its preaching; it is not mentioned in the *kerygma*. This is so because at the centre of the church's preaching is the fact of the coming of the Messiah. A new age entered the world in Christ. Christian worship is the manner in which this new reality came to expression in the world; its purpose was not the individual sanctification of believers but the creation of the people of God, the manifestation of the church as the life of the new age. Worship is not an end in itself, but the manifestation and anticipation in time of the coming day of the Lord, of the new creation.

Here we see the primary difference between Christianity and the mystery religions. In the mystery religions the cult is primary; reality is defined in terms of the cult. In Christianity

4

what is primary is the historical action of God in Christ, the worship or cult of the church having reality only in so far as the historical fact is acknowledged. Thus Christian worship was not understood as a repetition of the saving events in which it was and is grounded. These events are unique and unrepeatable. Christian worship is the proclamation, the showing forth, of these saving events for the world. Baptism is a 'likeness' of the death and resurrection of Jesus Christ (Rom 6:5). It is a likeness of the death and resurrection of a believer considered as member of the body of Christ. In baptism Christ does not die and rise again. Instead, the Christian is united with a new life created by the unrepeatable events upon which baptism is grounded. Like the Eucharist, it manifests their power.

However a changed understanding Christian worship came about through the changed place of the church in the world. This is not to say that it was due entirely to the events associated with the conversion of Constantine. Joseph Jungmann has shown, for example, how the church's struggle with Arianism had a profound effect on the way in which Christ was regarded in the prayers of the church.[2] The process was far more complicated than the effect of a single event.

In the situation after Constantine, with the Edict of Milan, Christian religious freedom is understood as the freedom of the cult. The identification of Christian worship as a cult gave a new meaning to it. The church's struggle against the cult reached its peak as it attempted to absorb the masses of people in the empire for whom the pagan cult was an organic part of their relationship with nature. But this struggle against paganism could not be limited to a negative thrust such as its condemnation of idols. The church had to fill up the empty space created by the expulsion of the cult. The church took upon itself the function of sanctifying those areas of life which

---

2.   See *The Place of Jesus Christ in Liturgical Prayer* (New York: Alba House, 1965).

had previously been served by paganism. In order to convert the world the church took on the function of a cult.

This may be illustrated by looking at the place of the building in relation to Christian worship. We know that the teaching of Jesus and the apostles transposed the idea of 'temple' from a sacred place to the living reality of the person of Christ and his people as the place where God met with God's people and they with God. The place of worship in pre-Constantinian Christianity played no special role at all. The building's significance was instrumental; it was simply the place where the church gathered.

Clearly there is an anti-temple element in Stephen's speech in Acts 7. For a long period Christians were deprived of the opportunity to build churches even if they wanted to, but it would be a mistake to explain the absence of buildings simply on external circumstances. In the centre of the faith of the early church was the understanding of the church as a living temple, experienced in the Eucharistic assembly. But beginning with Constantine a change occurred in the development of the life of the church's worship and its view of the church building. The church building became freed of its subordination to the Eucharistic assembly and acquired an independent significance of its own. The centre of attention shifted from the church assembled, to the church building itself as a sanctified space or building, a place for the habitation and residence of the sacred and so capable of sanctifying whoever entered it. Church buildings were constructed which took account of two important cultic notions, on the one hand the acceptance of the ancient idea of a temple memorial raised over the tomb of a martyr or saint, and on the other hand a temple built at the place of a theophany. The Basilica style, which originally was the place of assembly for the performance of the state cult, gradually assumed the function for both types of sacred place.

This development in the life of the church, its absorption of many aspects of the cultic understanding of worship into its own, consequent on its changed status vis-à-vis the empire, had an important effect on understanding the locus or place of theological reflection in the church. One may appreciate the significance of these effects by considering how divergent ecclesiologies give rise to divergent dogmas.

That the liturgical context of theological thinking is important in discussion of the person of the Holy Spirit may be indicated by how respective ecclesiologies relate to the work of the Spirit. Statements about the Spirit that arise in this specific context assume that the coherence of their theological truth derives from and is addressed to the God before whom the statements are made. They presuppose the setting of theology in the context of prayer. Such a view would see 'mystery' as a positive and not a negative aspect of speech about God.[3] It is maintained for example that 'the doctrine of the Holy Spirit has been cut off from the doctrine of the church.' That whilst

> the Holy Spirit was given all honour and attention in the *De Deo uno et trino* in the *De Ecclesia,* He retained what could be termed without exaggeration a subordinate position. From being understood as the very life of the church, He came to be seen as a sanction and guarantee. Where authority was stressed as the formative principle of the church, He was presented as the guarantee of that authority. Where individual freedom was stressed against authority, He became the guarantee of such freedom. He acquired a clearly defined function within the church.[4]

---

3.   See E Jüngel, *God As the Mystery of the World,* transl of *Gott als Geheimnis der Welt* (Grand Rapids: Eerdmans, 1983), 250ff.

4.   A Schmemann, *Church, World, Mission* (New York: St Vladimir's, 1987), 185; cf R S Komyakev, 'On Western Confessions of Faith', in Schmemann, *Ultimate Questions: An Anthology of Modern Russian Religious Thought* (New York: St Vladimir's, 1977), 50ff; *Orthodox Ethos — Studies in Orthodoxy,* vol 1, A V Philippou ed, (Oxford: Holywell, 1964), 78ff.

This protest from the East against both Catholic and Free Church ecclesiologies presupposes a view of the locus of ecclesial life in a union with God in which the being and life of the church comes to expression as communion and unity with Christ, existing as community in history. Consequently, the East's view of ecclesiology finds its deepest teaching 'about the church without teaching the church as a separate subject in itself'.[5] A close link is seen here between the ecclesiological reality, understood as mystery, and the Holy Spirit in the mystery of the Trinity. As a consequence the task of theology within this context is understood as a human work of reflection which, 'in both its intention and its actual content must bear witness to the holy presence of God who reveals himself in the Son by the power of the Spirit'.[6] It is, in fact, grounded in the life of the worshipping community and 'undertaken in the very presence of God'.[7]

It is precisely because of this insistence on the relationship between thought and being as a consequence of the triune God's saving action, celebrated in the liturgical life of the ecclesial community, that the Eastern church found it necessary to formulate a dogmatic basis for union with God. It brought to the surface the tensions which had existed between Western and Eastern Christian traditions from earliest times, tensions concerning the primary nature of the church's union and communion with the God understood as holy Trinity.[8] These tensions focus in the addition of the *filioque* to the ecumenical creed and in the Palamite controversy.[9] Both disputes revolve around similar issues concerning the way in which the creature is united with the Creator. Both East and West had increasingly

---

5.   A M Ramsey, *The Gospel of the Catholic Church* (London, 1956), 146.
6.   A Phillippou, *Orthodox Ethos, op cit,* 73.
7.   *Ibid.* See also J Zizioulas, *Being as Communion* (New York: St. Vladimir's, 1985), 116.
8.   See J Zizioulas, *op cit,* 70ff.
9.   See below.

divergent answers to this question. We now turn to an exploration of this divergence in order to illustrate both the issues in which this divergence comes to expression in theological form, and to elucidate the parameters in which ecumenical dialogue concerning the foundational confession of the Christian faith, the mystery of the blessed Trinity, may fruitfully be continued.[10]

The current discussion of the proposal from the World Council of Churches that 'all churches should revert to the original text of the Nicene Creed as the normative formulation' and thus excise the *filioque*, presents churches with a unique opportunity for extensive re-examination of fundamental theology.[11]

As has already been indicated, one of the difficulties which such a proposal presents is that the unexamined assumptions by which theology proceeds in the East and the West often peremptorily preclude dialogue. According to Vladimir Lossky,

> The difference between the two conceptions (East and West) of the Trinity determines the whole character of theological thought . . . The difference is such that it becomes difficult to apply the same name of theology to the two different ways of dealing with divine realities.[12]

Again, from a quite different perspective, dealing with what is perceived to be the East's attitude to the *filioque*, no less a theologian than Karl Barth expresses incomprehension that Eastern theologians can find the *filioque* responsible for such doctrines as the immaculate conception and papal infallibility!

---

10. For the following see G Watson, 'The *Filioque*—opportunity for debate? *Scottish Journal of Theology* 41, 1988: 313ff (included in this volume).

11. *Spirit of God, Spirit of Christ — Ecumenical Reflection on the Filioque Controversy*, L Vischer ed, (London: SPCK, 1981), vi.

12. V Lossky, *In the Image and Likeness of God* (London: Mowbrays, 1974), 80.

On the other hand Barth sees the *filioque* as essential and the East's denial of it as tantamount to tri-theism.[13]

If we as Westerners are to come to terms with the issues raised by the East's objection to the addition of the *filioque*, there are certain basic aspects of their approach to the spiritual life of the Christian and to the church as the locus of theological reflection which we must understand.

Karl Rahner has observed that in western theology the doctrine of the one God, as distinct from the Trinity, assumed primary importance. From the point of view of the East this could only be understood in terms of a certain theological sickness. The Trinity in the West became locked in splendid methodological isolation. We speak, Rahner says,

> of the necessary metaphysical properties of God, but not of God as experienced in salvation history in his free relations to his creatures. For should one make use of salvation history, it would soon become apparent that one speaks of him whom Scripture and Jesus calls Father, Jesus' Father, who sends the Son and who gives himself to us in the Spirit.[14]

The problem to which Rahner draws attention has deep roots in the history of dogma and the relationships between Eastern and Western theologies from the time of the ancient church.[15]

---

13. K Barth, *Church Dogmatics*, 1/1 (Edinburgh: T&T Clark, 1936), 551ff.

14. K Rahner, *The Trinity* (London: Burns & Oates, 1970), 18.

15. Perhaps the quintessential Protestant formulation of the problem is that of Schleiermacher; see 'On the Discrepancy between the Sabellian and Athanasian Method of Representing the Doctrine of the Trinity', *The Biblical Expository and Quarterly Observer* vol 1, No xix, 1835: 1ff, especially 69ff. Here Sabellius is supported by Schleiermacher precisely because he rejects the view that the ontic differences involved in the history of the economy of salvation enter into the definition of the Trinitarian hypostases. See also F Schleiermacher, *The Christian Faith*, *op cit*, Section 170, 738ff, where the methodological irrelevance of the Trinity in theology is

If we look at St Basil's defence of the deity of the Spirit in his work *De Spiritu Sancto*,[16] we are immediately struck by the fact that his argument has its form and structure determined by his understanding of the content and form of the divine liturgy.[17] It is therefore not without significance that Basil indicates the liturgical setting of the dispute which he addresses.[18] Those who question the Holy Spirit's deity maintain that, since the preposition 'in' of the liturgical ascription 'in the Spirit' predicated creaturely circumscription of him who by nature is uncircumscribed, the Spirit could not be said to be equal with the Father. The latter is implied by the preposition 'with' in other ascriptions contained in the liturgy.[19]

Basil replies that the opponents' thinking has failed to take account the primary distinction, presupposed by the liturgy, between God's essence or *ousia* and the hypostatic economy which takes place for the creation and reconciliation of the creature.[20] The former cannot be thought of as divided or circumscribed in any sense, so Basil allows his opponents' protest against any division which could introduce polytheism

---

deduced from the fact that it assumes 'a distinction in the Supreme Being' (*ibid*, 739). 'It (the Trinity) can never be an immediate utterance concerning Christian self-consciousness' but only 'a combination of several such utterances' (738).

16. *The Library of Nicene and Post-Nicene Fathers*, vol viii, P Schaff and H Ware eds, (Grand Rapids: Eerdmans, 1984).
17. It is unfortunate that Rahner, *op cit*, 18 n 13, proceeds to categorise Greek thought as 'formalistic', without seeking the reason for their reluctance to inquire about hypostatic relationships in God's essence. It consists in their determination to understand the Trinity on the basis of the economy of salvation which takes place so that the creature may be renewed as a creature, not that God's essence may be revealed.
18. Basil, *op cit*, Section 1 3.
19. *Ibid*, Section 4 6.
20. *Ibid*, Section 5 7.

into the church.[21] God's essence is incomprehensibly undivided; but on that account Basil does not deny that such words as 'of' and 'through' and 'in' are properly predicated of God. The church recognises, he says, both aspects: the ineffable undivided unity of God's essence, and the hypostatic economy expressed in words which imply local movement.

Here we see at least two things which are of importance in Basil's argument and in appreciating his theological method.

1. God's relationship with the world is understood in terms of the specific historical content of the history of salvation in which the trinitarian hypostases are active for the creation and reconciliation of the world.

2. The relationship between the hypostases and God's undivided essence is understood in terms of an ineffability which, celebrated in the doxological ascriptions of the liturgy, is directly proportional to the voluntary nature of God's condescension to the creature in its created contingency, expressed in the economy of salvation.

The theological importance for St Basil of this distinction between the trinitarian hypostases and the ineffable unity of God's essential being cannot be over emphasised. It derives directly from, and gives expression to, the basis of the liturgical celebration of the creature's ontological renewal by God's free action in Christ through the Spirit. Therefore, to predicate prepositions applicable to the economy of salvation, for example, 'through' and 'in', of God's *ousia* or essence is to call into question the very basis of the church's life, celebrated in the liturgy. It questions the free, voluntary and therefore mysterious nature of God's condescension in the economy of salvation for the creature's sake. Such questions make the very reason for the church's doxology a cause for dividing God's being. For the economy did not take place that God's being

---

21. *Ibid,* Section 5 and 6.

might be added to, but that the creature might be renewed as a creature.[22]

Basil's theological method gives rise to highly paradoxical language. He speaks of the Spirit

> as impassibly divided, shared without loss or ceasing to be entire . . . to everyone who receives it, as though given to him alone, and yet it sends forth grace sufficient and full for all mankind.[23]

This kind of language and the structure of Basil's argument are a direct result of the basically liturgical locus of his argument. Statements are made which, while referring to God in quite distinctive and logically incompatible ways, derive their coherence from the fact that they express an action which is at one and the same time an existential experience of the worshipping community. Here theological coherence can be expressed only if the unexpressed condition of the doxological statements is fulfilled. This is that the theologian is the recipient of the free grace of the Holy Spirit who in Christ unites both God and the creature, and persons with other persons in the fellowship of his body.

Consequently, in the perspective of the Eastern church any discussion of the Holy Spirit in the mystery of the Trinity cannot be divorced from the question of how the creature is united with God's life in and through God's acts of creation and recreation, celebrated in the liturgy. For the mystery of the creature's participation in God involves an ineffably free action of God which is correlative with the ineffability in which the triune God's essence is undividedly one.[24]

---

22. *Ibid*, Section 8 18: 'Shall his care for us degrade to meanness our thoughts of him?'
23. *Ibid*, Section 9 22.
24. It was the need to formulate a dogmatic basis for union with God which impelled the Eastern church to formulate teaching on the distinction between God's essence, energies and hypostases. On this important issue, one which lies beyond the scope of this

Linguistically, it is important to note that in Basil's argument there are those statements which refer to God's ineffable individual unity—in the sense in which 'with' is ascribed to the Spirit with the Father and the Son. These statements are concerned with God, as distinct from God's activity,[25] who performs the deeds of creation and redemption with a freedom that corresponds to the ineffability of God's nature. They are doxological in form, that is to say, they are statements in which

> the otherwise usual sense of the word is surrendered in its being used to praise God—the word is released from the manipulation of our thought and we must learn ever anew from the reality of God what the word properly means .[26]

On the other hand there are those statements which serve as the basis of the church's doxological ascriptions; these fall into the category of what Basil calls *kerygma*, and refer to the tradition concerning the historical witness to the acts which constitute the economy of salvation.

---

paper but is of critical significance in any ecumenical encounter, see J Zizioulas, *Being as Communion* (New York: St Vladimir's Press, 1985), 70ff; J McIntyre, 'The Holy Spirit in Greek Patristic Thought', *Scottish Journal of Theology* 7, 1954: 374, and *The Shape of Pneumatology* (Edinburgh: T&T Clark, 1997); V Lossky, *The Mystical Theology of the Eastern Church, op cit*, 70ff; G Florovsky, *St Gregory Palamas and the Tradition of the Fathers*, Sobernost, Series 4, No 4, 1961: 186ff; R C Walls, 'St Gregory Palamas', *Scottish Journal of Theology* 21, 1968: 435ff; L Meyendorf, *A Study of Gregory Palamas* (London: The Faith Press, 1964).

25. The question of the legitimacy of such statements about God, understood in this way, is argued in the debate between H Gollwitzer, *Die Existenz Gottes im Bekenntnis des Glaubens* (Munich: Chr. Kaiser Verlag, 1964), ET *The Existence of God* (London: SCM, 1965), 202ff, and E Jüngel, *Gottes Sein ist im Werden* (Tübingen: J C B Mohr, 1967), 5.

26. W Pannenberg, *Basic Questions in Theology*, vol 1 (London: SCM, 1970), 216.

The structural difference between these two sorts of statements is not amenable to logical correlation of one with the other. This is precisely what Basil's opponents attempted to do. The history of Jesus is the subject of didactic tradition and witness; Jesus Christ, true God and true Man, is the subject of doxological ascription. From the confession 'true God and true Man' we cannot adduce or give theoretical explanations of the historical events of Christ's humiliation and exaltation. Serious logical problems, which soon become theological problems, arise once these statements are abstracted from the *Sitz im Leben* of the liturgy, which presupposes the celebration of the ontological renewal of the creature by God's free action in history.

To prevent this confusion, to which God's opponents had succumbed, Basil enjoins, 'Dogma is to be observed in silence', and 'the meaning of dogma is difficult of understanding for the very advantage of the reader'.[27]

We note then in Basil's argument a direct relationship between a correct understanding of theological reflection and what is celebrated in and presupposed by the liturgy. To impugn the Spirit's deity, to dispute the doxological ascription 'with' as implying the mystery of the Spirit's ineffable unity with the Father and the Son, is at once to call into question the historical content of the hypostatic economy of the Son, God's being made man, which is predicated of the Spirit. It is thus to deny the mystery of the creature's salvation celebrated in the liturgy. The congruence of the mystery of the Holy Spirit, in relation to the unity of God's triune life, with the mystery of our

---

27. Basil, *op cit*, Section 27.76; cf D Bonhoeffer, *Christology* (London: SCM, 1966), 27: 'To speak of Christ means to keep silent; to be silent is to speak. The proclamation of Christ is the church speaking from a proper silence . . . We must study Christ in the humble silence of the worshipping community'. See also the discussion in E Thurneysen, *Die Lehre von der Seelsorge*, 5th edition (Zürich: Theologischer Verlag, 1980), 93ff.

redemption is posited by Basil as the basis of true theological knowledge.

We can further illustrate the issues raised by St Basil's concerns in his defence of the deity of the Holy Spirit, particularly his assumption that in the liturgy the creature's participation in the Spirit of God is the ontological ground of its renewal as a creature. With a view to directing the discussion to problems associated with the differing assessments of the way in which the Holy Spirit is understood in the East and the West, we now turn briefly to the Palamite controversy and a contemporary interpretation.[28]

The reference to the Palamite controversy derives its significance from the fact that in Gregory's debate with Balaam he was confronting the classical Western distinction, in its Thomist form, between created and uncreated grace. We may recall that the dispute was occasioned by Gregory's defence of the monks on Mount Athos who claimed that they experienced the uncreated light manifested in Christ's humanity on the Mount of Transfiguration. Balaam denied this and asserted that it was not uncreated but created light. Gregory saw this as a fundamental challenge to the participation of the creature in the divine life as a consequence of the incarnation and the gift of the Spirit. The reality of the Eastern church's notion of deification was called into question.

Palamas' development of the doctrine of the divine energies, the *energeia*, is based on a tradition which goes back to the foundational work of Maximus the Confessor. Basically, it is the distinction between the union of God with God's self (natural union), union of God with the creature in the economy (hypostatic union), and union between God and the creature in creation and reconciliation, (union according to the *energeia*).

---

28. See the excellent discussion of the issues related to the Palamite controversy in D Reid, *Energies of the Spirit: Trinitarian Models in Eastern Orthodoxy and Western Theology* (Atlanta: Scholars Press, 1997).

The latter two kinds of union, hypostatic and according to the energies, are achieved by God's will, not by God's nature. The *energeia* proceed from God as the means by which God relates God's self as Father, Son and Holy Spirit to that which is not God. The incarnation is the union of the second person of the Trinity with the creature for the sake of its union and communion with God through atonement and reconciliation. As a consequence of the active and passive obedience of Christ, an obedience achieved for our sake in the Spirit, Christ becomes the mediator of a new humanity as the head of a new humanity. The gift of the Spirit to the church is to be understood as mediated by Christ, and the union between God and the creature achieved by and in the Spirit is participation in the ontologically renewed humanity of the ascended Christ. A distinction, however, is maintained between Christ and the church by understanding the union of the church with God in Christ according to the *energia* and not a repetition of the hypostatic union. The mission of the church is to call creation to participate in its created vocation fulfilled in Christ's restoration of the relationship between God and creatures, and between creatures and creation. This cosmic dimension of Christology, as distinct from the anthropologically centred concerns of the Western tradition's fascination with guilt based on legalistic contractual notions of sin, is an important aspect of the difference between Eastern and Western notions of the work of the Holy Spirit.

We can illustrate the above point from a different perspective and a more contemporary context. The issues related above are discussed in Eric Mascall's book, *Existence and Analogy,* where he attempts a neo-Thomist defence of the doctrine of analogy as a theological method for expressing the God/creature relationship. It is a defence against Vladimir Lossky's criticism of St Thomas on the basis of the Palamite view of the divine energies and the creature's union with God.

Mascall holds that for Thomas being is not a *genus* since there is nothing outside it from which it may be differentiated.[29] What is true of beings in their relationship with one another must be true of the relationship between God and things. But since being is not a *genus* the relationship between God and creatures must be one which can be spoken of only analogically, as opposed to univocal or equivocal predication. Thomas distinguishes between two fundamental types of analogy, that of 'two to a third' and 'one to another'. The latter, for obvious reasons, is the only type appropriate to God. For God cannot be compared with something else in which both God and the creature exist. The analogy of 'one to another' is divided into two further types, 'attribution' and 'proportionality.[30] In the former the predicate belongs formally and properly to one analogate, and only relatively and derivatively to the second. The analogy of proportionality rescues the analogy of attribution from being simply an assertion that, if creatures are then God is. By thus co-joining the analogies of proportionality and attribution the transcendence as well as the immanence of God in relation to the creature can be held together. The difference between the mode of signification and the thing signified, in terms of existential judgments formed about created nature, grounds theological use of analogical predication in speech about God.

But the problem with Mascall's argument is that it assumes a relationship between God's nature *per se* and the creature *qua* creature.[31] Either the relationship presupposed by Thomas' doctrine of analogy is a relationship of the creature to God's essence, and therefore the creature is seen to have a natural relationship with God. Or the relationship between God and the creature is not divine and therefore is finite, and the creature ceases to be! In order to avoid these alternatives Mascall resorts to a distinction which destroys the basis of the analogy of

---

29. E Mascall, *op cit*, 99ff.
30. *Ibid*, 101-103.
31. This issue is discussed in V Lossky, *The Mystical Theology of the Eastern Church, op cit*, 76ff.

attribution upon which he attempts to rescue Thomas' doctrine of analogy. Mascall maintains that God is not given to the creature in a finite mode but that the creature 'participates God in a finite mode'.[32] The finitude is not that which is participated, but the mode of participation.

But the problem here is that the basis of Thomas' analogy of attribution is a direct relationship between the being of God and the being creature, albeit in a creaturely form. To introduce another analogy of proportionality into the basis of the analogy of attribution is to destroy the ground of analogical predication as a means of speech about God in relation to the creature. For the actual finitude of creaturely existence, the discrepancy between the relationship between its essence and its existence, as compared with God's, is the basis of the analogy of attribution. Mascall contends against this argument that it is intolerable that in God's relation to the creature any distinction should be drawn between God's relation to the creature and God's relation to God's essence!

> God and his essence cannot be separated. If the energy communicates God it communicates his essence.[33]

We have used this discussion of Mascall and St Thomas vis-a-vis the East to illustrate the difficulty of speaking effectively about the God/creature relationship so that due regard is held for both God's freedom and therefore for the mystery of God's existence and the participation of the creature in God's life. The problem focused in the person of the Holy Spirit.[34]

The issue of the creature's participation in God as celebrated in the liturgy is a question that is in contention not only in the

---

32. *Op cit*, 151.
33. *Op cit*, 152.
34. See on this K Rahner, *The Trinity, op cit*, 1-30. The same problem could just as well be illustrated by Barth's Christology and his defence of the *filioque*. See also the articles in this volume on the *Filioque* and on the soteriology of Barth and Anselm.

relationship between Eastern Orthodoxy and the Catholic West, but also between traditions which derive from the reformation of the church in the sixteenth century—the Lutheran and Reformed traditions.

In teaching what later become known in the controversies between the Lutherans and the Reformed as the *extra Calvinisticum*,[35] the Calvinist extra, Calvin sought to emphasise several things. First, that Christ is mediator of creation and redemption, secondly, that Christ is not known according to the way he is in himself, as one with the Father and the Spirit, but in the way in which he is for us, 'clothed with the Gospel'. This is the same distinction that the Eastern church makes between union according to nature or *ousia* and union according to the energies of the holy Trinity.

The basis of Calvin's claim for the relationship between creation and redemption, allowing for the continuities and discontinuities presupposed by God's act of reconciliation, is the fact that God's relationship to the world is mediated in creation and redemption by the one Christ. He is not revealed to us in terms of his inner divine glory, which he shares with the Father and the Spirit as ineffable divine life, but as God in Christ clothed with the gospel. Therefore the relationship God establishes with the creature by Word and Spirit does not relate to God's being and freedom as such. It relates to Christ and the Spirit who 'accommodate' themselves in humility to the lowly estate of the creature, so as to raise it in order to renew it according to its created purpose. This means that for Calvin the created structures of Christ's human reason and experience become the means God uses to communicate God's self in acts of gracious union and communion.

---

35. See E David Willis, *Calvin's Catholic Christology: The Role of the So-called Extra Calvinisticum in Calvin's Theology* (Leiden: E J Brill, 1981).

Consequently, Calvin's pneumatology arises from an acknowledgment of Christ's active and passive obedience, whereby the whole work of his incarnation and the establishment of the church is the fulfilment of God's purpose for creation in relationship to himself. For example, in contrast to the prophets Christ received the Spirit without measure, not for his own sake, in and for himself. He is by nature ever one with the Spirit. He receives the Spirit for our sakes in order to sanctify in himself the flesh of our fallen human nature which he assumed from Mary.[36] It is this aspect of Calvin's pneumatology that forms the basis of the dispute between the Reformed and the Lutheran churches with respect to how one understands, theologically, the presence of Christ in the Eucharist.

This voluntary self-emptying of the Son of God is the basis of the reconstituting act whereby, through the obedience of the second Adam, the wilful disobedience of the first Adam is replaced in the humanity of Christ for our sake. Likewise, Calvin believes that Christ's humanity was not relinquished by his ascension. For Christ did not need exaltation as the Son of God; he is ever one with the Father and the Spirit. He was and is exalted for our sake. He never ceased to be God and to rule the universe. He was exalted according to his manifestation for sinners as their High Priest.[37] God the Father has appointed Christ 'heir of all things' (Heb 1:2) according to his accommodation to our lowliness, not according to his eternal divinity.

---

36. 'I sanctify myself that they may be sanctified in truth' (John 17:19); cf Calvin's *Commentary on Luke* (1:15) and *Institutes* 2.13.2, and his *Commentary on John* (16:15) where Calvin distinguishes between Christ's 'hidden and intrinsic power' and 'that office which he has been appointed to exercise toward us'.

37. *Institutes* 2 13 2; cf *Commentary on Hebrews* (5:7).

Calvin's use of what later became known as the *extra Calvinisticum* ensured that he was able to give theological significance to the relative theological and ethical judgments that we are called upon to make as Christians, and non-Christians, without compromising the freedom of God's grace. This relates to one of the central questions of the Reformation debates—the issue of human free will in relationship to God's grace. For Calvin the relationship between God and the creature established in Christ takes account of the relativities of the human situation. This situation has been and is mediated by the person of Jesus Christ who accommodates and continues to accommodate himself through the Holy Spirit to the created modes of our existence as the means whereby he wills to exercise his rule in the church and the world. The focus of theological coherence for Calvin is thus this-worldly and cosmic in its nature and scope.

On the other hand Luther's understanding of the presence of Christ in the church and the world is surrounded by a strong dialectic in order to safeguard the freedom and Lordship—the grace of God—in God's relationship with the creature. Luther's rediscovery of the doctrine of *simul justus et peccator* meant that the whole of his theology was cast in a dialectic inherent in this understanding of the gospel of God's grace. In a wealth of expressions Luther employs, we see how important this is to the coherence of his theological thought. *Regimen spirituale/regimen corporale, regnum gratiae/regnum rationis, regnum fidei /regnum operum, regnum Christi/regnum Caesaris, Hörreich/Sehreich;* the two kingdoms are not two magnitudes excluding each other or competing with each other for rule, but two overlapping aspects of the one invisible kingdom of God. The kingdom of God assumes a dual aspect within the world, and each aspect is inseparable from the other whilst history lasts. Ultimately, eschatologically, there are not two kingdoms but one, God's kingdom. But it is of the utmost importance to distinguish the two kingdoms in this world of time and space, the world of fallen creation. To confuse the two kingdoms was a great mark of the anti-Christ. That may be brought about by the subordination of the spiritual kingdom to the worldly kingdom as amongst the Turks or, vice versa, with the Pope. What the devil does in either case is anticipate the last judgment of God by decisions made in this world, and that is the essence of sin. It is the refusal of faith and grace, which is the essence of the gospel. The sharpness of the strife created by the gospel in its conflict with the world, inherent in the *simul iustus et peccator* dialectic, meant that Luther had little sense of the new creation in Christ as an already accomplished fact.[38] Luther's doctrine of temptation (*Anfechtung*), which corresponds with his view of faith, means that the believer has difficulty learning to live on the resurrection side of the cross.

There is a continuing controversy amongst Lutheran theologians as to the possibility of and the nature of a third use of the Law, apart from its negative functions of restraining evil and convincing of sin. This is a sign of an on-going question as to whether the severe dialectic entailed in Luther's understanding of the Christian life as *simul iustus et peccator* is sufficient to present the rich texture of God's purposes in Christ for the renewal of creation.

The differences alluded to in this discussion between Reformed and Lutheran churches are of a piece with those indicated in the discussion of the issues of the Palamite controversy in the West. Both relate to the God/creature relationship and how that relationship can be given theological

---

38. But see the development of a new interpretation of Luther's understanding of Christ's presence in the believer's life in Carl Braaten and Robert Jenson eds, *Union With Christ: the New Finnish Interpretation of Luther* (Grand Rapids: Eerdmans, 1998).

coherence, whilst at the same time maintaining the integrity of God's transcendence and the creature's creatureliness. We started by indicating how St Basil understood this relationship in the context of the experience of salvation, celebrated in the Christian liturgy. The manner in which pneumatology develops will be dependent upon how the factors which condition this experience and give it structure are incorporated in theological reflection and dogmatic formulation.

The work of the Spirit in relation to Christ and the church derives its missional and cosmic perspective from the fact that Christ as the mediator of creation with the Spirit did not cease to be such as the eternal Son of God manifested in the flesh. It is the one Word of God who orders unfallen creation and reconciles rebellious creation. Consequently, the mission of the church relates not merely to the announcing of a static state of affairs based on God's judgment revealed in Christ, relating willy-nilly to all people. Rather, it participates in the same continuing economic condescension of God which forms the basis of its life and mission. For God in Christ not only now providentially rules and preserves his creation, but through his Word and sacrament deals with people in the Spirit so that they come to express their true humanity as the vocation of all created things (Rom 8:19ff). The church's worship and mission are the epiphany of Christ's continued condescension to incorporate his people in the Spirit in his creative and reconciling work.

Karl Barth and St Anselm's Theological Program

It would be difficult not to agree with the judgment of Barth himself concerning his Anselm book; that, although of all his books he had written it with the greatest love, in America and Europe it was of all his books the least read.[1] This is somewhat surprising, considering what is thought by most commentators to be the decisive influence of this book on the formulation of Barth's dogmatic method from 1931 onward. This is after the critical turn which Barth made subsequent to the publication of his first systematic attempt, *Die christliche Dogmatik im Entwurf*.[2] This paper attempts to assess how Barth understood Anselm's theological program and in what respects this understanding evinces a characteristic systematic weakness in Barth's own theological project.

When Barth's work on Anselm appeared, the apparent novelty of his exposition caused both theologians and philosophers to take sides on the question of his exegesis.[3] Barth contended that Anselm does not attempt to demonstrate

---

1. K Barth, 'Parergon', *Evangelische Theologie* 8, 1948: 172.
2. Chr Kaiser (München: Verlag, 1927). That Barth was not unacquainted with St Anselm at this time is evident from his contention in *Die christliche Dogmatik*; he finds him lending support for the view that God is known only through God; we do not know him, but in him we are known (96-8, 102, 108).
3. Cf E Gilson, *Sens et nature de l'argument de saint Anselme. Archives d'histoire doctrinale et litteraire du Moyen Age* 9 (1934). Gilson maintains, contra Barth, that St Anselm's Name for God expresses an essence, a content of thought (7, n 1). An analysis of this content is sufficient to prove God's existence. Cf Barth, *Anselms Beweis der Existenz Gottes im Zusammenhang seines theologischen Programms*, 2 Aufl (Zürich: 1958). ET *Anselm: Fides Quaerens Intellectum* (London: SCM, 1960), 75.

by means of an 'independent' proof any article of the Credo which he affirmed to be true in faith, but simply demonstrated by means of a proof how such affirmations are true.[4] Here Barth sees the idea of *ratio* as of decisive importance in understanding the relationship between faith and knowledge.[5] This relationship within a theological context is called the *ratio fidei*.[6]

In correlation with what Barth understands as Anselm's doctrine of truth, the relationships between all the different uses of *ratio* are conditioned by the fact that for Anselm the Word of God is the *ratio veritatis*.[7] As distinct from all noetic and ontic *rationes* the *ratio veritatis* is not Truth because it is *ratio*, but is *ratio* because it is Truth.

> The following holds good for all those other *rationes*
> *with* which the *ratio Dei* is not identical but which as
> the *ratio* of his creation participate in the *ratio Dei*:
> Truth is not bound to it but it is bound to Truth.[8]

The truth of any noetic *ratio* is dependent upon its correspondence to the ontic *ratio* for the establishment of the veracity of its concepts and propositions; under no circumstances can it be conceived to be creative.

> Thus from time to time in the event of knowing, it
> happens that the noetic *ratio* of the *veritas* conforms to
> the ontic and to that extent is or is not *vera ratio*—or
> (and this is normally the case *in praxi*) is to some
> extent *aliquatenus*. Fundamentally, the *ratio* either as
> ontic or noetic is never higher than the Truth but
> Truth itself is the master of all *rationes* beyond the

---

4.   K Barth, *Anselm, op cit*, 60-62. Cf H Bouillard, *K Barth*, Part Two: *Parole de Dieu et existence humaine* (Paris: Aubier, 1957), 146.

5.   K Barth, *Anselm, op cit*, 44.

6   *Ibid*, 46.

7.   *Ibid*.

8.   *Ibid*, 48.

contrast between *ontic* and noetic, deciding for itself, now here, now there, what is *vera ratia*[9] Because Truth disposes of all *rationes*, the revelation of Truth must be in the form of authority. The human capacity for reason itself becomes a *vera ratio* when it conforms to this something that is dictated.[10] This is not to be understood as a sacrifice of intellectual integrity, but the only possible and ultimately rational attitude one can assume before the authority of the believed but hidden *ratio* of the Object of faith.

> The antithesis between *auctoritas* and *ratio* does not coincide with the difference between God and man but represents the distinction between two stages of one divine road along which man first attains faith and (but now *sola ratione*) attains knowledge.[11]

Barth sees that the necessity of faith's search for understanding, the point of departure for theological knowledge, resides in the nature of the *ratio* of the Object of faith, not in the inquiring human intellect as such. Faith and understanding could never be opposed in Anselm's thought, or conceived in terms of a higher or lower form of knowledge.[12]

Whether *intelligere* is achieved by the believer or not, there is no question of the result of the quest raising doubts about the existence of *fides*, since it is only in faith that humans can begin to understand the outward authority, the Object of faith. The phenomenon of the fool who denies the existence of God poses the question for Anselm of the possibility of unbelief in the light of the Object of faith.[13] The *insipiens* question can be understood only within the context of faith since

---

9.   *Ibid*, 47.

10. *Ibid*, 48.

11. *Ibid*.

12. Contra R Prenter, 'Glauben und Erkennen bei K Barth', *Kerygma und Dogma* 2, 1956: 156ff; and 'Die Einheit von Schöpfung und Erlösung', *Theologische Zeitschrift* 2, 1946: 161ff.

13. K Barth, *Anselm, op cit,* 160; cf H Bouillard, *op cit,* 161ff.

> Anselm's proof works on the assumption that there is
> a solidarity between the theologian and the worldling
> which has not come about because the theologian has
> become one of the crowd, or one voice in a universal
> debating chamber, but because he is determined to
> address the worldling as one with whom he has at
> least this in common—theology.[14]

Anselm therefore sees the fool within the precincts of the church.[15] The fool's position in view of the power of the objective *ratio* of the object of faith that is enlightened by the *summa veritas*, must be seen in the last analysis as absurd and taken with a certain sense of humour.[16] There is no other way to address the unbeliever than as a sinner who is reckoned not to have sinned.[17]

Barth's Exposition of St Anselm's Proof for the Existence of God

Barth interprets Anselm's presentation of the name of God, with which he conducts his proofs, in close relation to what he has taken to be the self-grounded nature of the *summa veritas* which we have encountered in his understanding of the relation of *fides* to *ratio* and *intelligere*. The formula, 'that than which nothing greater can be conceived',[18] must not be interpreted from the point of view of any possible conception derived from human experience of this world. 'It is deliberately chosen in such a way that the object which it describes emerges as something completely independent of whether men in actual fact conceive it or can conceive it.'[19] Its emergence as the divine name is meant to draw attention to an essentially unexpressed

---

14. K Barth, *Anselm*, 68.
15. *Ibid*, 70.
16. *Ibid*.
17. *Ibid*.
18. *Ibid*, 123.
19. *Ibid*, 74.

condition. This is that it indicates 'nothing about the nature of God, but rather lays down a rule of thought which, if we follow it, enables us to endorse the statements about the nature of God accepted in faith as our own necessary thoughts'.[20] The formula must be understood as a strictly noetic rule in that 'it contains nothing in the way of statements about the existence or about the nature of the object described'.[21]

This last point is crucial with respect to Barth's interpretation, in particular the relationship between chapters II and III of the *Proslogion*. For the moment it is sufficient to note that, by emphasising the strictly noetic content of the proof, Barth does two things which have importance for his understanding of the doctrines of Revelation and of God in the *Church Dogmatics*. Firstly, he holds that since the revealed name of God is a strictly noetic rule the existence of God is not derivable from any idea of God's nature. God is known wholly in the event of God's self-revelation or not at all, since God is who God is in the event of God's self-revelation. Secondly, Barth stresses the fact that the historical distinctions, which are involved in God's self revelation in history, do not, as such, enter into the meaning of the relationship between these distinctions and revelation. Rather the ontic distinctions involved derive their meaning from their relationship with the *summa veritas*.

Therefore the revealed name of God can establish only a 'strong and discernible'[22] connection with revelation and the existence of God; it cannot be used as a basis for an analysis of the nature of God. For, strictly speaking, God is not a content of thought at all.[23] From this it must be concluded that the

---

20. *Ibid*, 80.
21. *Ibid*, 75.
22. *Ibid*, 76.
23. Cf H Bouillard, *op cit*, 150: 'Dieu ne ressemble à rien, n'appartient à aucun classement conceptuel. C'est tout autrement qu'il faut entendre

'presupposition of this Name has without doubt a strictly theological character'.[24] The objection which may be brought, that St Anselm's Name is simply an expression of a human desire to express the inexpressible, and consequently it has no more meaning than this particular desire,[25] fails to realise that the incomprehensibility of the Name is defined by the revelation of God. It is precisely because God is the revealed God that God is the veiled or incomprehensible God. The whole point of the proof is to raise this incomprehensibility of God from being an article of faith to the level of understanding its necessity in terms of the Object of theological knowledge.[26]

The same argument is applied when Barth suggests that the divine Name is merely a *vox*. Barth points out that Anselm had declared in *Proslogion* I: *Non tento, Domine, penetrare altitudinem tuam . . . sed desidero aliquatenus intelligere veritatem tuam.*[27] This *aliquatenus* cannot signify 'a quantitative limitation of the range of human insight into the nature of God simply because this Name of God is lacking in ontic content'.[28] The lack of ontic content means that God can be known within the sphere of faith alone, in which the *ratio* of the Object of faith can be conceived in a manner appropriate to it. Hence the words used in this specific context and determined by this known but inconceivable Object become, in the guise of mere words, the divine revelation. It is with respect to this characteristic that the proof offered by Anselm in *Proslogion* II and III is to be understood as superior to the proof offered in the *Monologion*.[29]

---

l'idée de Dieu: non l'essence s'offrant au regard de l'homme, mais la désignation de l'essence: aliquid quo maius cogitari potest . . .'

24. K Barth, *Anselm, op cit*, 26.
25. Anselm, *Apologetic in Reply to Gaunilon's Answer in Behalf of the Fool*, chapters iv & v (in *Anselm: Basic Writings*, [La Salle: Open Court, 1962], 159ff; 161ff).
26. K Barth, *Anselm, op cit*, 79ff.
27. *Ibid*, 83.
28. *Ibid*.
29. *Ibid*, 84, 86-8.

In the *Monologion* Anselm had arrived at the formula, variously expressed, but meaning in substance that God is that which is greater than all.[30] Such a formula, precisely because of its implied relationship to contingent, factual, non-necessary things, was incapable of rigorous demonstration. The formula of the *Monologion* meant that it was, in fact, quite possible to conceive the factual non-existence of God. The form of the proof offered in the *Proslogion*, precisely because of its strict noetic character, excludes its dependence upon the existence of things in general and indicates that the area in which it is intelligible is wholly dependent upon the determination of the *ratio* of the Object of faith. The exclusion of ontic content from the formula found in the *Proslogion* corresponds to the fact that Anselm demonstrates the existence of the free, self-sufficient God who in grace stoops to reveal God's self to the creature. This change in the structure of the *Proslogion* proof means that there is no longer a separation between *essentia* and *esse*, potentiality and actuality, in understanding the existence of God.

> God is all that he is, not through participation in certain potentialities, not identical with his actual Power; all his potentialities do not first require to be actualised in the reality of his Power, but he is himself what he ever is and what he ever is, he is himself.[31]

The same kinds of considerations are brought to bear by Barth in the distinction he draws between the nature of the proofs in *Proslogion* II and III. In chapter II, Anselm is understood to be concerned to establish that, since the fool conceives something when he hears the divine Name, and what he conceives exists in the knowledge of what he conceives, the God of the revealed

---

30. *Ibid*, 84, note 4.
31. *Ibid*, 94. The influence of this aspect of Barth's interpretation is seen clearly in his attitude to natural theology. This latter, on the basis of a general concept of being, attempts to divide God's potentiality from his actuality; see K Barth, *Church Dogmatics* 2/1 (Edinburgh: T&T Clark, 1957), 63ff, 85ff.

Name cannot be conceived as existing in the mind alone but also in reality. There is implied the extramental existence of God.[32] For Anselm believes that to exist extramentally is greater than to exist in the intellect alone.[33] This proof, which asserts that a being's extramental existence is greater than an existence *solo intellectu*, does not identify the being who is thus conceived as greater because extramental. It simply recognises the possibility of such an existent being *in intellectu* and *in re*. Nothing has been proved except the conclusion that it is impossible, if God exists, for God to exist *solo intellectu:* God must exist also *in re*.

> The positive statement about the genuine and extramental existence of God (in the general sense of the concept 'existence') does not stem from the proof and is in no sense derived from it but is proved by the proof only in so far as the opposite statement about God's merely intramental existence is shown to be absurd.[34]

It is because Anselm's argument in *Proslogion* II has a general idea of existence in mind, and consequently an ontic content that is not presupposed by the Object of faith, that Barth calls it a 'general proof' for the existence of God.[35] It may be true that what we know as actually existing in the mind and in reality we cannot at the same time conceive as existing and not existing. But it is possible to conceive a state of affairs in which that which is thus known does not exist, or is no longer existing; the hypothetical denial of its existence is not absurd. The reason why this is so is the general concept of existence with which the proof operates. Thus the proof can have only the negative value indicated above, unlike the proof of *Proslogion* III which

---

32. K Barth, *Anselm, op cit,* 123.
33. *Ibid,* 125.
34. *Ibid,* 128.
35. *Ibid,* 100.

excludes even the hypothetical non-existence of the Object of the proof.

There is therefore in *Proslogion* III no statement about God's existence in terms of the existence of things in general analogous to what we find in chapter II, which includes human's own conception of themselves as existing. St Anselm is not Descartes.[36]

> Out of the general *vere esse* there now arises significantly before us a *vere esse* whose reality has its basis neither merely subjectively nor merely subjectively and objectively but is based beyond this contrast *a* se, in itself.[37]
>
> The nerve of the proof is seen to consist in what it denies rather than in what it asserts. By what this revealed Name forbids, God is distinguished from all things whose existence can possibly be conceived as non-existent. Therefore the proof must be seen in a very specific context.
>
> If an article of faith, fixed in itself as such, has been proved in such a way that the opposite statement would be reduced *ad absurdum* by means of the statement of the Name of God which is likewise assumed to be revealed and believed . . . *Intelligere* means to see into the noetic rationality and therefore into the noetic necessity of the statements that are revealed, on the basis that they possess ontic rationality and necessity as revealed statements, prior to all *intelligere*, to all proof and therefore not based on proof.[38]

---

36. *Ibid*, 139; cf K Barth, 'Schicksal und Idee in der Theologie', *Theologische Fragen und Antworten. Gesammelte Vorträge*, Bd 3 (Zürich: Verlag AG, 1957), 78-81.

37. K Barth, *Anselm, op cit*, 141.

38. *Ibid*, 143f.

That God's existence is subject to proof in this unique way is shown further, according to Barth, by the way in which Anselm constructs his proof by means of an address to God in the form of a prayer. God therefore stands over against the human knower seeking understanding by means of this proof, 'not as an "it", not even as "he", but as "thou", as the unmediated "thou" of the Lord'.[39] This factor conditions not only the believer's understanding of the noetic necessity of faith in relation to its Object, but also the believer's thinking and speaking about created reality. For, 'along with his existence, he also has his thinking about existence, its values and degrees, all entirely from the Creator'.[40]

The 'fool' who fails to achieve understanding by means of the revealed Name is to be considered neither as a rational nor as a moral defective, but simply as a fool.[41] He accomplishes that which in the light of God's unique existence it is 'forbidden to attempt'.[42] This attempt by the fool has its theological parallel in the sinner's attempt to justify him/herself over against the unconditional grace of God in Jesus Christ.[43] The fool is one who cannot appreciate, at the decisive point, the inexpressible freedom of God in God's movement toward the creature. By this fact the fool is simply revealed to be a fool. But it needs to be emphasised at once that if, as a believer, Anselm

---

39. *Ibid*, 151.
40. *Ibid*, 152.
41. *Ibid*, 159f, 165.
42. *Ibid*, 159.
43. *Ibid*, 160. There is an obvious relation here to Barth's understanding of the fool and his view of sin as *das Nichtige*; cf K Barth *Church Dogmatics* 3/3 (Edinburgh: T&T Clark, 1960), 327ff. This aspect of Barth's thought, which has given rise to criticism of its universalist direction, springs directly from his doctrine of God. This has generally not been appreciated. Cf G C Berkouwer, *The Triumph of Grace in the Theology* of *K Barth*, (London: Pater Noster Press), 262ff; J Baillie, *Our Knowledge of God* (London: Oxford University Press, 1939); H Hartwell, (London: Duckworth, G, 1956), *The Theology of K Barth*, 186-87.

reaches understanding of God's unique existence by means of the revealed Name, then he too must see himself as one who now understands, as being in exactly the same position as the fool. The epistemological implications of the freedom of God's election in Jesus Christ have this effect for both the fool and the believer.

> It is only by grace that Anselm's solidarity with him (viz the fool) has been ended. The *insipiens* thinks and speaks as one who *is* not saved by the grace of God. That is the reason for his perversity, and why he can say *Deus non est*. The reproach does not imply any uncharitableness. It is with just this reproach on his lips that Anselm takes his place as near as it is possible to be, and therefore with as much promise as there could possibly be, alongside this fellow mortal whose action is so unintelligible.[44]

The proof of *Proslogion* III expressed as a noetic rule takes into account the implications, in the area of epistemology, of Barth's view that the doctrine of election is an integral part of the doctrine of God.[45] The lack of reference to ontic factors not presupposed by the event in which God reveals God's self corresponds to the freedom and majesty of God who, in choosing to be God, chooses the human creature in God's Son from all eternity in Jesus Christ. The proof of the noetic rule in *Proslogion* III, therefore, is one which presupposes the event of divine revelation in which human thinking and willing is unconditionally determined by the freedom of God's movement toward the creature. God is both Object and Subject in the event of revelation in which God is who God is for the creature. The only rational response the creature can make in understanding the world and the self is one which

---

44. K Barth, *Anselm, op cit*, 160.
45. *Ibid*, 158-61; cf K Barth, *Church Dogmatics* 2/2 (Edinburgh: T&T Clark, 1957), 132f.

assents to the Name of God as an article of faith and presupposes it for all that follows—it is able to illumine the noetic necessity of faith . . . by the roundabout route of ontic necessity which is inseparable from ontic rationality. Thus theology can know what is believed, that is, prove it.[46]

Assessment of Barth's Interpretation of St Anselm's Proofs

We take up the question of Barth's interpretation with particular reference to the relationship which he establishes between Proslogion II and III. We recall that Barth had distinguished between them and found the latter to be superior to the former in so far as it lacked reference to any relationship between God and the creature which was not presupposed by God's self-revelation. The proof in Proslogion III excludes reference to any ontic factor. It thereby assumes that the question raised by God's revelation concerning God's existence is one which can be meaningfully asked only in the context in which the same revelation determines the structure of the event in which God makes God's self known, and so allows for the absolutely free nature of God's condescension to the creature. It does not ask if or how God's existence is proved, but in what way it is proved.

But Barth is also concerned to show that the proof of *Proslogion* II is really on the way to the proof of Proslogion III. The conclusion of Proslogion II that God cannot exist in the understanding alone but *in intellectu and* in *re* rests, Barth asserts, on the ground that

> The positive statement about the genuine extramental existence of God (in the general sense of the concept of existence) does not stem from the proof and is in no sense derived from it but is proved by the proof only in so far as the opposite statement about God's merely

---

46. K Barth, *Anselm, op cit*, 83f.

intramental existence is shown to be absurd . . . If that
is a 'proof' then it is a proof of an article of faith which
still holds good apart from all proof.[47]

Barth's view is that the proof of Proslogion II concludes in a
negative statement to the effect that if God exists, God could not
do so in thought alone. But the positive statement upon which
this negative statement rests, which refers to God's unique
existence, does not have its origin in this general proof.

H Bouillard, in an analysis of St Anselm's proofs,[48] concedes
Barth's general point that in the argument found in *Proslogion* II
Anselm proceeds negatively and indirectly, by way of reduction
to the absurd. The proof of *Proslogion* II is limited to showing
the internal contradictions involved in the denial of existence to
a Being such that no greater could be conceived. However,
Bouillard insists, in arguing so Anselm wishes to derive a
positive conclusion, albeit in a negative form, namely, the real
extramental existence of such a Being. Bouillard maintains that
the fool understands the formula expressing the divine Name in
Proslogion II, and this possibility is open to anyone who reflects
upon the temporal and supra-temporal nature of things. For
example, in Anselm's reply to Gaunilo's answer in behalf of the
fool, he stresses the fact of the meaningfulness of the formula in
Proslogion II by relating it to reflection upon things which are
more or less good.[49] What is implied by Anselm's procedure,
understood in this way, is that it is incumbent upon the
unbeliever to show that the propositions of faith which Anselm
is attempting to understand are meaningless. The unbeliever
has to show that not merely within our experience we do not
compare things absolutely, as greater or more perfect, but that it
is necessarily the case that things are not greater or more perfect
in this sense. He would thus be forced by Anselm's argument to

---

47. *Ibid,* 128f; cf 132f.
48. Bouillard, *Parole,* 158 ff; see also the same author's *Connaissance de Dieu* (ET *The Knowledge of God* [London: Burns & Oates, 1969]).
49. *Apologetic,* ch viii; *op cit,* 161ff.

say that the things within our experience are necessarily the only things and that the notion of God is meaningless by definition.[50] It would appear that Barth has methodological reservations which preclude his appreciation of this side of Anselm's argument. He underplays the importance of the rational infrastructure of human language in arriving at the meaning of the proofs.[51]

The position adopted by Barth in his exposition of the proofs implies a structural hiddenness of revelation which has methodological implications for theology. It entails that the rationality of human thought-forms and language is dependent upon their correspondence to the structure of the event of God's self-revelation. All the distinctions and relations presupposed by the event of revelation, to which the rationality of the creature can be related, of which Bouillard had assumed a common rational structure to apply to believer and unbeliever alike, Barth understands exclusively within the context of the event of revelation and the nature of the God who is there revealed. Since in revelation we have to do with an act and not a state of revealedness, speech about God cannot be separated from that event in which the revealed God's nature and existence coincide. Therefore 'the man outside the church, the man who is without revelation and faith, knows nothing in actual practice of him who bears the Name'. But given the event of revelation which includes the reality and possibility of human knowledge of God, the church actualises a possibility which, though open to all, is hidden from them by the fall and

---

50. Cf J N Findlay, 'Can God's Existence Be Disproved?' in *New Essays in Philosophical Theology,* A Flew and A MacIntyre eds, (London: SCM, 1955), 55ff.

51. Cf T F Torrance, 'The Problem of Natural Theology in the Thought of K Barth', *Religious Studies* 6/2, 1970: 121ff. See also, T F Torrance, *K Barth, Biblical and Evangelical Theologian* (Edinburgh: T&T Clark, 1990), 136-159.

the concrete mystery of God's election.[52] Thus at any given time Barth can distinguish between knowledge of God that is validly an inference from the structure of worldly reality in the event of revelation, as the believer seeks to understand what he believes, and that which is invalid:

> Here within the church, there takes place a *conicere*, an inference from experience of the world as to the nature of God just as truly as this does not take place outside the church.[53]

We shall conclude by indicating the decisive shift which Barth's study of Anselm produced in his way of doing theology. Our analysis will concentrate on what Barth regards as the 'heart' of dogmatics, the doctrine of reconciliation.[54] However, we should indicate that the structure of Barth's doctrine of revelation, which forms the substance of the first volume of the Dogmatik, is conditioned by the lessons he had learned from Anselm. As distinct from *Die christliche Dogmatik,* where the starting point had been the situation of the preacher and the hearer, in the *Kirchliche Dogmatik* Barth relates the determination of the ontic forms of revelation, the event nature of revelation, Scripture and proclamation, and the noetic determination of the creature as the recipient of revelation, to the nature of the Word of God. Thus section 5, *The Nature of the Word of God,* is the link between sections 3-4 and 6-7.[55]

With respect to Barth's doctrine of reconciliation we first of all note its dependence, in terms of its structure, upon the way Barth understands God to have acted.[56] There is no question of presupposing the church's understanding of dogma by a

---

52. K Barth, *Anselm, op cit,* 116f.
53. *Ibid,* 117. This interpretation is indebted to E Jüngel, *Gottes Sein ist im Werden,* 2 Aufl (Tübingen: Mohr, 1967).
54. K Barth, *Church Dogmatics* 4/1 (Edinburgh: T&T Clark, 1956), 3.
55. K Barth, *Church Dogmatics* 1/1 (Edinburgh: T&T Clark, 1936), 141ff; 51ff; 98ff; 213ff; 284ff.
56. K Barth, *Church Dogmatics* 4/1 (Edinburgh: T&T Clark, 1956), 128.

possibility related to an abstract view of the nature of God. The reality and possibility of doctrine resides in the being and act of God who is revealed in Jesus Christ. Therefore the divinity of the Mediator is understood by asking after the possibility posited by the reality of Jesus Christ as God for human beings, how this one 'takes part in the event which constitutes the divine being'.[57] From the way in which God is related to human beings in Jesus Christ we must conclude that 'in this way, in this condescension, he is the eternal Son of the eternal Father . . . This is how God is God'.[58] The outward form of the event reveals the 'inward divine event'.[59] The humanity of Jesus is therefore that which corresponds to this inward divine event. As man Jesus can only be understood in the light of the fact that, 'as true God, ie, the God who humbles himself, Jesus Christ is this true man, ie, the man who in all his creatureliness is exalted above his creatureliness'.[60]

Barth's understanding of the doctrine of the two natures of Christ, divine and human, shapes his view of the doctrine of the two states of Christ, humiliated and exalted.[61] The historical distinctions implied by the earthly life, death, resurrection, ascension and reign of Christ are to be understood in terms of the structure of the event of revelation in which God is God.

> We have not spoken of the two states (*status*) of Jesus Christ which succeed one another, but two sides or directions or forms of that which took place in Jesus Christ for the reconciliation of man to God . . . his one work, which cannot be divided into different stages or periods of his existence, but which fills out and constitutes his existence in this twofold form.[62]

---

57. K Barth, *Church Dogmatics* 4/1 (Edinburgh: T&T Clark, 1956), 129.
58. *Ibid.*
59. *Ibid.*
60. *Ibid*, 131.
61. *Ibid*, 132ff.
62. *Ibid*, 133.

If the divinity and humanity of Christ are to be understood in terms of aspects of the nature of the Word of God to human beings, aspects of their involvement in this event and its relationship to the creature are to be understood as a third dimension of the same Word of God. If the being of Jesus Christ is to be understood in terms of God's self-determination for the creature and the creature for God's self, then the relationship of the creature to this event is to be seen from the point of view of the unity of this two-fold determination of God.[63] This third aspect of the doctrine of reconciliation, as that which expresses the inconceivable unity of God's being as Word and Act, is the *summa veritas* of all ontic and noetic *rationes* involved in God's revelation to the human creature.[64] Therefore the resurrection in its relation to the historical life of the man Jesus must be seen in the fact that

> God willed to give to his eternity (ie, the Son in relation to the Father) with him and therefore to himself an earthly form. He willed to give to the inner secret radiance of his glory an outward radiance in the sphere of creation and its history. He willed to give to his eternal life space and time.[65]

The fact that according to the New Testament Jesus was raised from the dead by the Spirit confirms for Barth that the historical life and obedience of Jesus do not enter, as such, into the definition of the nature of the event. Since

> the fact that Jesus Christ was raised from the dead by the Holy Spirit and therefore justified confirms that it pleased God to reveal and express himself to the crucified and dead and buried Jesus Christ in the

---

63. *Ibid*, 136.
64. *Ibid*, 147-48; 151-52; 202-204.
65. *Ibid*, 308.

unity of the Father with the Son and therefore in the glory of the free love which is his essence.[66]

Barth structures the doctrine of reconciliation, under the general heads of Jesus Christ the Lord as Servant, the Servant as Lord and the True Witness. This corresponds to his analysis of the nature of the Word of God[67] and, since this analysis serves as the basis for the dogma, of the doctrine of the Trinity.[68] It is for this reason that Barth could not accept the interpretation of the proofs of St Anselm given by Bouillard, for that could only be seen as an attempt to consider the rationality and necessity of the revealed Name apart from the possibility which its reality posits. Any postulate which presupposes a freedom of the creature, either to know or to obey God, that does not correspond to the reality and possibility presupposed by the actual freedom of God to be who God is, in God's own eternal self election actualised in Jesus Christ as the God of the creature, finds no place in Barth's thought. It is methodologically excluded.

---

66.   *Ibid*, 309.
67.   K Barth, *Church Dogmatics* 1/1 (Edinburgh: T&T Clark, 1936), 150ff; 162ff; 184ff.
68.   *Ibid*, 349ff.

St Anselm's Soteriology and Karl Barth's Theological Method

Recent discussion of St Anselm's theology of reconciliation[1] has again raised the question of freedom in respect to the relationship presupposed between God and humans in this encounter.[2] It has been asked whether, in fact, St Anselm's account excludes God's ability to act freely, 'within the dynamics and development of the narrative',[3] and suggested that such exclusion derives from an understanding of God's 'unchanging nature beyond the influence of persons and events within the narrative'.[4]

In a similar fashion Karl Barth[5] objects to St Anselm's exposition found in *Cur Deus Homo*.[6] Through an examination of these objections we intend to show how Barth's difficulty with St Anselm's presentation indicates a systemic problem in Barth's methodology which undervalues the importance of the historical humanity of Jesus in the action of the atonement. We have previously argued[7] that Barth's interpretation of St

---

1. See M Root, 'Necessity and Fittingness in Anselm's Cur Deus Homo', *Scottish Journal of Theology* 40/2 : 211ff.
2. See also G Aulen, *Christus Victor* (London: SPCK, 1953), 101ff; J Denny, *The Christian Doctrine of Reconciliation* (London: Hodder and Stoughton, 1917), 75ff.
3. Root, *op cit*, 229.
4. *Ibid*.
5. K Barth, *Church Dogmatics* 4/1 (Edinburgh: T&T Clark, 1956), 485ff.
6. Quotes will be taken from the text of *Cur Deus Homo* translated by S W Dean, in *Anselm: Basic Writings* (Lasalle Illinois: Open Court, 1962).
7. See the essay in this volume, G Watson, 'K Barth and St Anselm's Theological Program', first published in *Scottish Journal of Theology* 30, 1977: 31-45.

Anselm's *Monologion* and *Proslogion* does not take into account Anselm's assumption of the importance of a common rational structure in thought and language existent between believer and unbeliever[8] as the basis for speech about God. This omission, consistent with Barth's view of the nature of revelation, affects the place and purpose of the trinitarian doctrine which is intended as the methodological *Urgrund* of the *Dogmatics*.

We will see in this connection that, in respect of St Anselm's exposition of soteriology in his later work, there is a 'close relation of St Anselm's soteriology with his general theology, not only in methodology, but also in essential subject matter'.[9] Consequently, we should expect to find a congruence in Barth's uneasiness with St Anselm's theology in this area as well.

Barth's objection to St Anselm's interpretation of the relationship between the incarnation and the atonement occurs within the context of his discussion of the nature of sin in the light of the revelation of God in Christ as the Lord who became a servant. In this light, Barth maintains, we see how God's word of forgiveness addressed to humanity shows that

> the corruption from which it calls and takes (man) consists in the fact that man is God's debtor. He is a debtor who cannot pay. God has to excuse him . . . Indeed, when we consider what the debt is, we see that no other action to it is adequate but the divine forgiveness![10]

Since humans' debt is of such a nature that they are in no position to pay, it must be concluded that God forgives humankind 'primarily and decisively because His forgiveness alone is the restitution of the right which has been broken by

---

8.   *Op cit*, 40, 41.
9.   J McIntyre, *St Anselm and His Critics* (Edinburgh: Oliver & Boyd, 1954), 185; cf 204.
10. K Barth, *Church Dogmatics* 4/1 (Edinburgh: T&T Clark, 1956), 484.

the sin of man'.[11] Barth therefore agrees with St Anselm's exposition of human sin as debt to God.[12] He finds St Anselm's presentation 'very accurate and complete'.[13] But Barth insists that God's revelation of human sin is at one and the same time its removal. Human guilt and debt towards God is revealed and removed by God's act of pardon.

> His (God's) forgiveness makes good our repudiation and failure and this overcomes the hurt that we do to God ... His forgiveness repels chaos.[14]

Consequently, on closer examination Barth finds St Anselm's exposition to be defective since

> he makes the remarkable assertion that it is not worthy of God to forgive man his sin *sola misericordia*, and therefore purely and absolutely and unconditionally. The divine forgiveness has to be thought of as conditioned by a prior satisfaction ... by restitution of that which man had stolen from God.[15]

Barth's concern here is to oppose any attempt to separate revelation as God's action from the action of the atonement, as if the sovereignty and effectiveness of God's action is conditioned by a prior claim of justice.

> Is there any event more serious or incisive or effective than that in which God forgives man all his sins? And does not the recognition of the divine decision in this event depend upon the fact that it is understood as pure and free forgiveness?[16]

---

11. *Ibid.*
12. *Ibid*; see Anselm's *Cur Deus Homo*, Book 1, chs xi, xii, xiv.
13. K Barth, *Church Dogmatics* 4/1 (Edinburgh: T&T Clark, 1956), 485.
14. *Ibid*, 486.
15. *Ibid.*
16. *Ibid*, 487.

It has been noted[17] that the appearance of *Cur Deus Homo* heralded a major departure from the conventional wisdom in the church regarding the nature of the atonement. The traditional view, carried along by the weight of St Augustine's authority, depicted the event in terms of a cosmic struggle between God and the devil. In this context the divinity of Christ came to the fore and humans were more or less helpless bystanders to the central drama.[18] In *Cur Deus Homo*

> the figure on the cross was seen with a new clarity to be that of a man. The devil slipped out of the picture and left God and man face to face.[19]

The atonement is not the consequence of a cosmic struggle between God and the devil, nor an arbitrary divine action, but the fruit of a personal choice. Christ is understood not merely as a passive instrument revealing a superior divine design, but as a willing agent, and as one who is so regarded by the Father. It is precisely this latter element, decisive for St Anselm's understanding of the atonement, which Barth finds so 'remarkable'. Barth's singular inability to appreciate Anselm's argument in this area of Christ's free choice and obedience as a human being illustrates the wider problem to which we have already alluded.[20] We refer to the significance of the historical particularity of Christ's humanity as that which in itself bears upon the definition of revelation. This fact in turn has serious

---

17. R W Southern, *The Making of the Middle Ages* (London: Arrow Books, 1959); *St Anselm and His Biographer* (Cambridge: Cambridge University Press, 1963), 93ff; J A Hopkins, *Companion to the Study of St Anselm* (Minnesota: University of Minnesota Press, 1972), 188ff.

18. Southern, *St Anselm and His Biographer, op cit*, 94.

19. Southern, *The Making of the Middle Ages, op cit*, 236; cf *Cur Deus Homo*, Book 1, ch vii, 187-89.

20. G Watson, *op cit*, 41.

consequences for Barth's understanding of the Trinity as the basis of his theological method.[21]

Barth finds evidence[22] to support his view that St Anselm construes the divine act of forgiveness as 'having to be conditioned before it can be accepted as a serious divine action',[23] against which Barth proposes 'the recognition of the divine decision in this event . . . as pure free forgiveness'.[24] But prior to the chapter which Barth cites, St Anselm had set out to prove that Christ's death was not the direct result of a divine command, but a free accommodation of the Son to the condition of humanity before God.

> The Father did not compel him to suffer death, or even allow him to be slain, against his will, but of his own accord he endured death for the salvation of men.[25]

Death as God's judgment upon human sin could not be demanded of one who was so purely good, if that one was unwilling to die.[26] If he dies it is because he voluntarily obeys the Father's will and surrenders himself to death. It is the Father's will that humanity should not be restored unless a greater thing be done in terms of God's honour than the dishonour which sin has incurred for God. The Son of God can therefore say that the Father desires his death inasmuch as the Son wills to suffer rather than that the whole human race should perish.[27]

It is important to note, against the tenor of Barth's criticism, that St Anselm is just as concerned as Barth to understand the

---

21. G Watson, 'The Filioque—Opportunity for Debate?' *Scottish Journal of Theology* 41/3, 1988: 330, 331 (included in this volume).

22. Anselm, *Cur Deus Homo*, Book 1, ch vii.

23. K Barth, *Church Dogmatics* 4/1 (Edinburgh: T&T Clark, 1956), 487.

24. *Ibid.*

25. Anselm, *Cur Deus Homo*, Book 1, ch viii, 191.

26. *Ibid*, Book 1, ch ix, 193ff.

27. *Ibid*, 196.

removal of sin as an act defined by God's decision and action.[28]
The difference between them arises with respect to the nature of
God's decision and action. For Anselm that decision and action
involves the fact that the Father 'was not willing to rescue the
human race, unless man were to do even as great a thing as was
signified in the death of Christ'[29]—God's decision is
understood in terms of the *a posteriori* actuality of the
incarnation and obedience of the Son of God. The 'precondition' to which Barth objects, and which in his view
mitigates against the atonement being understood on the basis
of *sola misericordia*, is seen to consist in Anselm's determination
to give full weight to the fact that here a human being had a
moral and spiritual struggle to achieve obedience to the Father's
purpose.

'Reason did not demand of another what he could not do,
therefore the Son says that he desires his own death.'[30] Reason
did not demand what, in view of the Son's sinlessness, was not
factually open to anyone else to accomplish. For no one else is
actually in a position of being, as a creature, under no obligation
to God. But the Son voluntarily assumes subjection to the law of
human obligation to God as a creature. It is the voluntary
nature of the Son's self-offering that is central to St Anselm's
exposition as opposed to considering the act of redemption
simply as a revelation of a divine decision. It is decisive for St
Anselm that here a human being endured a moral and spiritual
struggle for the world's redemption.[31] However, such emphasis
as St Anselm's gives this contingent factor as part of God's
action of atonement should not be seen as in any way
impugning consideration of such action as an action of God. In

---

28. J McIntyre, *op cit*, 40, 78, 203.
29. Anselm, *op cit*, Book 1, ch ix, 196.
30. *Ibid*.
31. Contra M Root, *op cit*, 222-24; cf Root's definition of God's aseity
     with the comprehensive exposition by J McIntyre, *op cit*, 167-71,
     175, 183-85, 190, 193.

this sense we now proceed to consider the background for such actions as are involved in the atonement being described as actions of God, as 'fitting' or 'unfitting'.[32]

St Anselm's Conception of Truth and Rightness

St Anselm's understanding of the relationship between God and the world, as this impinges upon his soteriology, is best understood by examining his views of truth and rightness.[33] It is here that we see the basis for his insistence that the atonement could not be understood as an act of God *sola misericordia*.

In attempting to show that every form of truth is a form of rightness St Anselm investigates right thoughts, upright willing, righteous actions, correct perceptions, and the straightness of material objects. This relationship and continuity in speech about divergent matters and things depends first of all on the presence in Latin of a single term which can be applied to all these cases, viz, *rectitudo*.[34] It is our intention to examine this concept as it elucidates the part played by the humanity of Christ in God's act of atonement.

For St Anselm, God is the Supreme Truth;

---

32. McIntyre, *op cit*, 162f, 166f, and L Hödl, 'Anselm von Canterbury', *Theologische Realenzyklopädie*, Bd 11 (Berlin: Walter de Gruyter, 1978), pp. 775-76; C R P Anstey, 'St Anselm Demythologised', *Theology* LXIV, 1961: 17ff.

33. Anselm, *Concerning Truth*, translated by J Hopkins and H Richardson (New York: Harper, 1967). Quotations will be of this text.

34. Anselm, *Concerning Truth*, chs xi and xii; cf R Campbell, 'St Anselm's Background Metaphysic', *Scottish Journal of Theology* 33, 1980: 317ff; H Bouillard, *The Knowledge of God* (New York: Herder & Herder, 1968), 83ff; Anselm, *Apologetic: A Reply to Gaunilon's Answer in Behalf of the Fool*, translated by S W Deane (Lasalle, Illinois: Open Court, 1962), ch viii.

there is truth in the essence of all that exists because
all things are what they are in the Supreme Truth.[35]
The Supreme Truth is the cause of all else that is said to be true,
both propositions and states of affairs.

> Although all the different kinds of rightness which we
> mention are what they are because the things they are
> in either are as they ought to be or else do what they
> ought to do, nevertheless the Supreme Truth is not
> rightness because it is under any obligation. All
> things are obliged to it, and it is obliged to nothing
> else.[36]

Truth has such an important place in St Anselm's thought as it
is integrally related to 'rightness'. The two words relate to the
same reality. Everything that is has a certain truth and rightness
which makes it part of an integrated complex of relationships as
a creation.[37] An important corollary of this is that any
creaturely thing, even though it may not possess a conscious
will, appears under an obligation to fulfil its truth or rightness.

---

35. Anselm, *Concerning Truth*, ch vii, 102; cf Campbell, *op cit*, 331: 'The
    notion of things as they ought to be is rooted in Anselm's
    background metaphysics, not only because it is required for our
    understanding of his treatment of truth, but also because the same
    notion plays a crucial role in the argument of *Cur Deus Homo'*.

36. Anselm, *Concerning Truth*, ch X, 108; cf chs i & xiii, also *Proslogion*,
    ch xiv, *op cit*, 21-22. See Campbell, *op cit*, 334ff. 'Things are what
    they are through the divine Word, and depend upon nothing else
    except the utterance of a word, or separate words, they are as it
    were a kind of language. That is why our words can be likenesses
    of them' (335). M B Foster, 'The Christian Doctrine of Creation
    and the Rise of Modern Natural Science', *Mind*, Vols XLIII, XLIV,
    XLV, 1934-1936: 446ff, 439ff, 1ff.

37. Anselm, *Concerning Truth*, ch xiii, 117; cf ch xii, 110f. See J
    Hopkins, *op cit*, 135; J McIntyre, *op cit*, 100. For the background to
    the philosophical question in dispute between Lanfranc and
    Berengar which was raging when St Anselm came to Bec, see
    Southern, *St Anselm and His Biographer*, 24ff.

This obligation is specifically related to its truth in relation to the Supreme Truth of all things.[38] This Supreme Truth, though it cannot be identified with anything particular, is that which allows us to say of this or that thing, state of affairs or proposition, 'the truth of that thing'.[39] Thus whilst St Anselm was aware of the characteristics that are peculiar to different categories of entities,[40] he wishes to emphasise that each thing stands under its respective obligation to the Truth. One can only know the rightness of things and persons when it is understood how they stand in relation to the Supreme Truth.

In Chapter 11 of *Concerning Truth,* St Anselm speaks through the disciple of things participating (*participando*) in the Truth.[41] But it should be noted that the idea of participation in the Platonic sense is not to be inferred from this. Anselm makes a key distinction between a thing's truth, which is understood as a right relation or state of affairs, and that which is the cause of truth. Just as the cause of a true proposition is not in the proposition itself, so a true proposition does not participate in its cause. Consequently, Anselm states emphatically that the Supreme Truth or Rightness is radically different from any creaturely truth and rightness.[42] The Eternal Son or Word is the Truth of created things,[43] not because he corresponds to the world but because he is its Truth.[44] Hence the necessary reasons which serve as premises by which Anselm demonstrates his arguments signify aspects of the exalted Truth, which remains exalted and beyond the grasp of the

---

38. Anselm, *Concerning Truth,* ch x, 108; ch xi, 109f; cf*Monologion,* ch 1, 38f.
39. Anselm, *Concerning Truth,* ch xii, 120.
40. Anselm, *Concerning Truth* ch v, 98ff, ch vi, 100ff.
41. Anselm, *Dialogus De Veritate,* MPL Tomus CLVIII, col 469: *nihil est verum, nisi participando veritatem.*
42. Anselm, *Concerning Truth,* ch. x, 108.
43. Anselm, *Monologion,* chs xxxiii, 95ff, xlvii, 111ff; *Proslogion,* ch xxiii, 28-29.
44. Anselm, *Monologion,* ch xxxi, 93.

human intellect, since its relationship to creaturely truth presupposes the freedom, the grace, of the will of the Creator Word.[45] St Anselm's demonstrations of the various articles of faith make more than simple logical connections. The demonstrations cohere because they correspond to factors which cohere in reality but which cannot be contained within the logic of the demonstration. Propositions or thoughts are not the cause of any truth.[46]

Propositions become true as they express the truth or rightness of things in relation to their proper order established by their coherence in the Truth of the Word of God. Consequently, the principle *credo ut intelligam* which appears as a methodological axiom in all of Anselm's works,[47] and not least in *Cur Deus Homo*, 'is a necessary precondition of intellectual comprehension of the Christian faith'.[48] Not only of the Christian faith and its doctrine, but also of any knowledge whatsoever of things, persons etc, in so far as it is understood that their truth, too, coheres in reality in the Supreme Truth. Anselm left indeterminate our knowledge of the exact character of this right relationship to the Truth of things, persons, etc. Although one may recognise that an entity exists rightly, one cannot fully describe or picture the right relationship involved. This is precisely because the relationship in question does not derive from a rational principle, but from the freely willed relationship between the Supreme Truth and its termination in

---

45. Contra R Prenter, 'Die Einheit von Schopfung und Erlösung', *Theologische Zeitschrift* 2, 1946: 66-167, 171; 'Glauben und Erkennen bei K Barth', *Kerygma und Dogma* 11, 1956: 76ff. Here it is argued that St Anselm's distinction between faith and understanding, which presupposes the distinction between the Supreme Truth and the truth of created things, tends to a neglect of the creaturely objectivity of the event of revelation, and that in this respect St Anselm is too dependent on St Augustine. Cf M Root, *op cit*, 218.

46. Anselm, *Concerning the Truth*, ch x, 108f.

47. McIntyre, *op cit*, 4ff, 55.

48. *Ibid*, 4.

a contingent order of creation which, while rooted and grounded in the Supreme Truth, has its own rationality and truth.

This is nowhere more obvious than in St Anselm's understanding of the necessity of Christ's incarnation in the *Cur Deus Homo*. Hence the truth of the creature which Christ assumes is no rational principle deduced from the nature of the Word. Rather, its teleology, as its truth, is established through the lived life of the incarnate Word which presupposes a voluntary and therefore an ineffable condescension.[49] The *tertium comparationis* in this relationship is thus not formal and logical, but what has been called

> a transition from being to act [in which] the formal logical levels become meaningful only at a point where they renounce their completeness and limit their process of formalisation in order that room may be left for the ontologic.[50]

Consequently, St Anselm's much criticised[51] rejection of simple forgiveness as the essence of the atonement will be seen to be grounded in his recognition of the gracious way in which God has dealt with humankind; in inestimable freedom accommodating God's self to the created truth of the creature's relationship to God in order to re-establish it in the truth *as a creature*. This is far removed from the view which deals with Anselm's thought as an exercise in logical necessity which

---

49. *Ibid*, 193: 'At the heart of Cur Deus Homo there is not rational necessity but Divine Grace'; cf 203f; contra Hopkins, *op cit*, 196-97 and Root, *op cit*, 227-30.

50. T F Torrance, *Theological Science*, 273. For Torrance it is by their relation 'to the Incarnation that our statements have their fundamental ontologic, for it is in the incarnation that our forms of thought and speech are grounded in God and yet earthed in the sphere of actuality where we live and move and have our being'.

51. Root, *op cit*, 224, 230; Barth, *op cit*.

grounds God's act in 'an unchanging nature beyond the influence of persons and events'.[52]

The Relationship Between the Incarnation and the Atonement

It will be recalled that, on the basis of his understanding of Truth and Rightness in created entities, St Anselm saw that their being who or what they were bore the marks of an obligation or debt to that which they were in the Supreme Truth. The relationship between creaturely and divine Truth was one which, though real, nevertheless involved the greatest disparity which was overcome by an act of will on the part of the Supreme Truth in which (whom?) all things cohere. This entailed creaturely truth being defined with the greatest possible logical openness.[53] It is our contention that St Anselm's emphasis on the voluntary nature of Christ's humiliation, the freely willed obedience of Christ in relation to his death, is intended to underline the fact that the divine and creaturely truths, while united by the ineffable condescension of Christ, are distinguished by the purposive teleology of Jesus' earthly life. Anselm's purpose in this was, on the one hand, to safeguard the actuality of the Son's humiliation as dependent upon God's free initiative.[54] On the other hand, in the light of

---

52. Root, *op cit*, p. 229.
53. Torrance, *op cit*, 273; cf T F Torrance, *Space, Time and Incarnation* (Oxford : Oxford University Press, 1969), and the important article by the same author, 'The Ethical Implications of Anselm's De Veritate', *Theologische Zeitschrift* 24, 1968: 309-319. See also, T F Torrance *The Christian Doctrine of God — One Being Three Persons* (Edinburgh: T&T Clark, 1996), 73-111.
54. McIntyre, *op cit*, 157. There seems to be no link made here between the hypostasis of the Son considered as an empirical entity involved in a moral and spiritual struggle and the voluntarily offered obedience of Christ. (See also on the same issue, 169.) This Nestorianising tendency in McIntyre is all the more surprising since McIntyre has seen the relationship in

this initiative of grace, he aimed to give full place to the actual obedience of Christ as a human being as that which re-establishes the creature as creature.[55]

For St Anselm the only reality in which it was possible to conceive sin as having occurred was that of the creature in its wilful failure in obligation to the Truth. God is obliged to no one. Consequently, if human sin is to be removed the Son must freely assume the form of a servant. The element of judgment that Anselm sees in the atonement derives from the fact that sin could appear to be under no law or obligation, and therefore like God, if the Son of God did not freely submit to judgment. God's justice and his mercy are therefore seen to be one through the obedience and death of his Son.[56] What Anselm had established in his analysis of Truth and Rightness and their relation to the Supreme Truth is seen in the *Cur Deus Homo* to involve the understanding of an integral relationship between the incarnation and the atonement, since it is possible to understand the fulfilment of an obligation to the truth only as a free act of the creature *qua* creature.

We also see that St Anselm's analysis of the voluntary humiliation of the Son of God for the sake of the creature's renewal as a creature is directly related to his understanding of his celebrated proofs for the existence of God.[57] Anselm's definition of the revealed name of God as 'that than which nothing greater can be conceived'[58] corresponds to his understanding of the relationship and differences between the

---

Anselm's argument between the voluntary nature of Christ's humiliation and Anselm's definition of God's aseity as the action of his grace (175, 183, 193). See also on this issue, Hödl, *op cit*, 775.

55. It seems incomprehensible that Aulen, *op cit*, 105, 148, should claim that Anselm, as an exponent of the typical Latin soteriology, should see no organic connection between the incarnation and the atonement!

56. Anselm, *Cur Deus Homo*, Book 1, ch xii, 203-204.

57. Anselm, *Proslogion*, chs ii & iii.

58. *Ibid*, ch ii, 7.

divine and creaturely truths and rightnesses established by the voluntary condescension of the Son of God and his obedience as a human being. The revealed name of God, expressing as it does the inconceivability of his non-existence as distinct from the conceivable non-existence of creaturely things,[59] opens up precisely the same discrepancy that is presupposed by the voluntary condescension of the Son of God who as a human being fulfils the creatures' debt or obligation to creaturely truth, since it is impossible to conceive the Supreme Truth as obliged to anyone.[60]

> By his action, then, Christ at one and the same time assumes created truth and rationality and makes them his own although he is distinct from them. As embodying in Himself the Supreme Truth God remains in a relation of freedom and transcendence and is not at our disposal.[61]

At one and the same time Christ is one with the Father and one with the creature, establishing by his free condescension the truth of God and the human being. If St Anselm were to follow Barth's suggestion and understand the act of atonement as *per se* an act of divine pardon, it would entail for him the destruction of the bases upon which he 'proves' the 'necessity' of Christ's death as a human being in *Cur Deus Homo*, and the existence of God in *Proslogion*.

We turn, in conclusion, to examine the argument St Anselm uses to show why 'it were not proper for God to put away sins

---

59.   See G Watson, 'K Barth and St Anselm's Theological Programme', 35f for the differences Barth sees between the proof offered in the *Monologion* compared to the *Proslogion*.

60.   Torrance, *Space, Time and Incarnation*, 65; cf St Cyril of Alexandria, *Scholia on the Incarnation of the Only Begotten*, Library of the Fathers of the Holy Catholic Church (Oxford: Parker & Rivingtons, 1881), 185ff, 190.

61.   Cf McIntyre, *op cit*, 162f, 166-68, 175, 193.

by compassion alone'.[62] Barth took exception to this thereby intending, as we have contended, to undervalue the part played by the human Jesus in the act of atonement. But first we intend now to take up, in confirmation of our interpretation of Barth, his reaction to S. Kierkegaard. In the congruence of negativity we elicit, from Barth's critique of Kierkegaard, are seen the same features to which he objects in St Anselm's presentation of the significance of the earthly humanity of Jesus. In this way it will be seen again how Barth is unable to appreciate the dynamic involved in revelation's ontic content, for methodological reasons.

Karl Barth and Soren Kierkegaard's Dialectic of Existence

Barth includes Kierkegaard in that category of theologians who attempt to bring the event of revelation into some kind of correlation with the believing person in terms of an independent anthropology.[63] Such theologies meet revelation with

> a self enclosed human reality beyond which there is nothing to confront it, and which, because it is itself the one and all, cannot be confronted by anything which might be identified with God who is distinct from man and the world and superior to both.[64]

Such a view must be called to order by showing that in revelation

> we pass beyond the limits of autonomous human self understanding, to a genuinely different level of thought when we realise that the conjunction 'God

---

62. Anselm, *Concerning Truth*, ch xii, 203.
63. K Barth, *Church Dogmatics* 3/2 (Edinburgh: T&T Clark, 1960), 21, 113-118; also *Church Dogmatics* 3/4, ix; and *Church Dogmatics* 4/1, 150ff, 740ff. *Epistle to the Romans* (Oxford: Oxford University Press, 1968), 10; 'Dank und Reverenz', *Evangelische Theologie* 7, 1963: 9ff.
64. K Barth, *Church Dogmatics* 3/2 (Edinburgh: T&T Clark, 1960), 119.

and man' or 'God with man' or 'man with God' means noetically and ontically that God *acts* towards man, and when we rigidly confine our view to the history which takes place between God and man.[65]

This means, in the particular relationship between humanity and God, that the structure of the relationship is not grounded in the relationship in which human beings stand either to themselves or other objects. So it is not a matter, where faith is concerned, of choosing between alternative ways of understanding oneself. The rationality of faith is grounded not in a possibility posited by the fact of human existence, but by the fact that

> With the divine No and Yes spoken in Jesus Christ, the root of human unbelief, the man of sin is pulled out. In its place is put the root of faith, the new man of obedience. For this reason unbelief has become an objective, real and ontological impossibility and faith an objective, real and ontological necessity for all men and for every man . . . This object of faith is, in fact, the circle which encloses them all and which has to be closed by every man in the act of his faith.[66]

Thus defined, the human act of faith, 'as this human act', has no 'creative but only a cognitive character'. It does not 'alter anything'.[67]

The decisive nature of Barth's rejection of Kierkegaard is directly related to the development of his trinitarian hermeneutic of revelation in the *Church Dogmatics*, consequent on his study of St Anselm.[68] Any suggestion that the act of faith could be understood apart from the act of revelation which posits its possibility in the inconceivable freedom in which God both elects humans and God's self, and which determines God's

---

65. *Ibid*, 124; see 125ff.
66. K Barth, *Church Dogmatics* 4/1 (Edinburgh: T&T Clark, 1956), 747.
67. *Ibid*, 751; cf 758-77.
68. K Barth, 'Parergon', *Evangelische Theologie* 8, 1948: 72, and G Watson, 'K Barth and St Anselm's Theological Programme', *loc cit*.

being as God in Jesus Christ as both One and Another in the unity of a Third, is excluded. For if the ontic and noetic relations implied in the object and subject of faith, considered in terms of their intra mundane existence, are not seen in the context of their reality and possibility as posited in the freedom whereby God posits God's self; then they, as ontic and noetic phenomena, presuppose a being with God which is not presupposed by God's being with the creature. For Barth that is impossible.

However, the consequence of Barth's attempt to understand the noetic and ontic factors involved in the subject and object of faith's inter relationship in terms of the inconceivable freedom whereby God posits God's self (as both One and Another in the unity of a Third), entails that they as noetic and ontic factors become as inconceivable as the inconceivability in which God posits God's self. So it is methodologically impossible to understand the historical action of God in Christ in terms of the creaturely reality which he assumed. The reverse, in fact, is the case. Truth of the creature is not understood as creaturely truth, on the basis of the distinctions involved by the Son of God's voluntary condescension to become this particular, contingent person, who is then related to God as a creature like other creatures. Instead, for Barth creaturely truth is correlated with the unities and distinctions in which God posits God's self as God. In St Anselm's terms this would be to make sin, as failure in obligation, predicable of the Supreme Truth.[69] Kierkegaard attempted to develop a method of understanding the Christian faith which sought to enter into dialogue with the factuality of the incarnation which presupposes, as an event in history, the 'becoming' of God. He wanted to elicit what kind of thought is

---

69. On Barth's understanding of knowledge of the creation as God's creation see *Church Dogmatics* 3/1 (Edinburgh: T&T Clark, 1958), 348-49. Cf E Jüngel, 'Die Möglichkeit Theologischer Anthropologie auf dem Grunde der Analogie: Eine Untersuchung zum Analogieverständis K Barths', *Evangelische Theologie* 22, 1962: 35ff.

appropriate to communicate the reality of God's being as 'becoming' in history. In his critique of Hegel's 'system', he showed how inappropriate any attempt to identify thought and being would be in appreciating the transition involved in any event's coming into being.[70] Hegel presupposed movement in the structure of thought itself. Kierkegaard, on the other hand, sought to distinguish between truth and logic.

> In logic the *becoming* proper to movement can have no place, logic *is*, and all that is logical *is* only, and it is this very limitation of logic which marks the transition from logic to becoming, where individual existence and reality emerge.[71]

So the problem of coming into being, the non-necessity of events as presupposing the freedom and contingency in which they came to be rather than not, entails that in knowledge of them as events this is taken into account. This knowledge requires an act of faith which acknowledges that such knowledge presupposes the freedom of the events having come into being. Consequently, historical events can never be considered as examples of logical sequences.

> Although that which has historically become is immobilised in the past and this is unchangeable, it is not for that reason a product of necessity. Its unchangeability only means that its real mode can no

---

70. On Kierkegaard's relationship to Hegel, see Kierkegaard, *Philosophical Fragments* (Princeton University, 1962), 12ff; H Diem, *Kierkegaard's Dialectic of Existence* (Edinburgh: Oliver & Boyd, 1959), 25ff. A similar critique in terms of scientific method is undertaken by M Polanyi, *Personal Knowledge* (London: Routledge, Kegan Paul, 1959), 65ff, 70f, 112-33, 265ff, *Knowing and Being* (London: Routledge, Kegan Paul, 1969), 140f, 174f, 177-79; see also the remarkable essay by M Heidegger, *An Introduction to Metaphysics* (Oxford University, 1959).

71. Diem, *op cit*, 18; Kierkegaard, *Philosophical Fragments, op cit*, 91-93.

longer be otherwise, but this does not exclude the possibility that it might have been otherwise.[72] In order to understand the type of movement involved in historical change Kierkegaard resorted to a category found in Aristotle and taken up in his own day by the philosopher Trendelenberg.[73] The category is *kinesis*. Kinetic thought attempts to find a mediating position between possibility and reality postulated by events coming into being. It attempts to understand the 'transition' of the movement in being's becoming. It entails a kind of a 'leap' which corresponds to the presupposed freedom in thought's object coming into being. Kierkegaard's idea of faith as a 'leap', therefore, has nothing to do with a kind of Promethean defiance, an irrational gesture, but defines the mode of rationality appropriate to the nature of events' becoming.[74] So faith is not an enquiry concerning potentiality as possible options open to God, but relates directly to the factuality of the 'becoming' postulated by the events associated with the incarnation of the Son of God. It is to safeguard this aspect of faith that Kierkegaard discouraged enquiry about the details of Jesus' historical existence. Such inquiry could easily become an attempt to dissolve the 'transition' involved in the thought of faith into a static ideal.[75]

Consequently, in a manner not dissimilar to St Anselm's principle of *credo ut intelligam*, in 'proving' the necessity of Christ's death in terms of the presupposed relational differential between creaturely and divine truth through the voluntary condescension of the Son of God, Kierkegaard maintains in his analysis of the event nature of the incarnation,

---

72. Diem, *op cit*, 27; Kierkegaard, *op cit*, 90ff, 95f, 103-105; M B Chamber, 'Was Jesus Really Obedient Unto Death?' *The Journal of Religion* 50/2, 1970; 121ff, 129f.
73. *Ibid*, 18, note 9.
74. *Ibid*, 89ff.
75. *Ibid*, 63f, 87f.

that the organ for the historical must have a structure analogous with the historical itself; it must comprise a corresponding somewhat by which it may repeatedly negate in its certainty the uncertainty of coming into existence. The latter uncertainty is twofold: the nothingness of the antecedent non-being is one side of it, while the annihilation of the possible is another, the latter being at the same time the annihilation of every other possibility. Now faith has precisely the required character; for in the certainty of belief there is always present a negated uncertainty, in every way corresponding to the uncertainty of coming into existence.[76]

We see the same kind of argument in St Anselm's defence of the freedom of Christ to choose to die in the light of prophetic statements concerning the necessity of his death. One can distinguish at least two kinds of necessity according to Anselm.[77] The first may be understood to entail 'A occurs because it is necessary that it should occur', secondly, 'It is necessary that B should occur because it occurs'. In the former the occurrence is a deduction from the necessity; in the latter the necessity is a deduction from the occurrence. The *Cur Deus Homo* sees the relation between prophecy and the death of Christ as consisting not of 'a prior necessity but of posterior necessity, because the death of Christ originates from his will and is freely chosen by him'.[78]

Barth's rejection of Kierkegaard's analysis of the nature of faith is of a piece with his rejection of St Anselm's understanding of the act of atonement as precluding its being understood as *per se* an act of God's pardon. This is the case because both St Anselm and Kierkegaard view the substance of the Christian faith as grounded in the particularity of an

76. Kierkegaard, *op cit*, 100f.
77. See McIntyre, *op cit*, 162ff.
78. *Ibid*, 163.

historical event which cannot be correlated to the being of God as such, without at the same time dissolving the creatureliness of the creature or the deity of God. The correlation between the historical and God, God and the creature, is understood only when the freedom of both is integrated by the life-act of Jesus considered as presupposing an ineffable condescension, understood from the point of view of the contingency of that life's human teleology.

On the other hand such factual occurrence as involved in Christ's becoming human can only be interpreted by Barth as presupposing the inconceivable act in which God posits God's self as both One and Another in the unity of a Third—the factuality of the teleology of the human life of Jesus becoming as inconceivable in terms of its historicity as the inconceivability of God's self-positing. Any other possible understanding of the factuality of Jesus' life-act is methodologically excluded by the nature of God's self-determination as God.[79]

Consequently, we find that Barth's rejection of Kierkegaard's exposition of faith's relationship to its object (subject!) brings to light aspects of his method which directly relate to his rejection of St Anselm's interpretation of the atonement in *Cur Deus Homo*. The exposition confirms our analysis of Barth's relation to Anselm in the congruence of arguments used by Barth to reject both Anselm's and Kierkegaard's understanding of the significance of the contingency and freedom of Jesus' life's work.

---

79. K Barth, *Church Dogmatics* 1/2 (Edinburgh: T&T Clark, 1956), 26-31; K Barth *Church Dogmatics* 4/1 (Edinburgh: T&T Clark, 1956), 287ff; H Ott, Der Gedanke der Souveränität Gottes in der Theologie K Barths', *Theologische Zietschrift* 12, 1956: 409ff.

The Necessity of Christ's Death

We turn, in conclusion, to consider the argument by which St Anselm demonstrates why 'it were not proper for God to put away sins by compassion alone'.[80]

The substance of Anselm's argument is that the voluntary nature of the Son of God's condescension for the sake of the creature presupposes an infinite disparity between the Supreme Truth and creaturely truth. Within this infinite disparity the teleology of Jesus' human life establishes the contingency and freedom of the creature in relation to the Supreme Truth. If God forgave sins by compassion alone, ignoring the significance of Jesus' life of obedience, sin, which originates in and can only be predicated of creaturely being and truth, would either be predicated of God or would remain unpunished and thus appear to be like God—under obligation to no law. This Anselm rejects, primarily because this is, in fact, not the way God has acted through the obedience of the Son of God as a human being.

That Barth signally fails to appreciate this point is shown by the way he deals with Anselm's argument consequent upon Boso's objection that:

> since God is free as to be subject to no law, and to the judgment of no one, and is so merciful as that nothing more merciful can be conceived; and nothing is right or fit save as he wills; it seems a strange thing for us to say that he is wholly unwilling or unable to put away an injury done to himself, where we are wont to apply to him for indulgence with regard to those offences which we commit against others.[81]

Barth holds that St Anselm

> thinks he can overcome this by saying that the freedom of God is inwardly conditioned by that *quod*

---

80.   Anselm, *Cur Deus Homo*, Book1, ch xii, 203.
81.   *Ibid*, Book 1, ch xii, 204f.

expedit aut quod decet, nec benignitas dicenda est, quae aliquid Deo indecens operatur. A God who willed to lie would not be God. Nor would a God who willed to forgive without the prior fulfilment of this condition.[82]

However, the fittingness of which St Anselm speaks is that of the way which God has actually taken in the act of atonement. The liberty of God and the creature is understood in terms of the way the Son of God has voluntarily assumed the creature's form for the creature's sake. That is why there is no liberty, *quod expedit aut quod decet;* because it is through the person of Jesus that God is obedient. And, since this in fact is how the matter stands in terms of the relationships and differences between the supreme truth of God and the contingent creaturely truth of human beings, it is impossible to say that God can lie; that is to say, act as though sin were subject to no law and like Godself was obliged to no one.[83] The basis of this impossibility is not an abstract theory about what God can or cannot do. To say that God cannot lie is therefore the same as saying, in the context of Anselm's argument, that the Son of God became truly human for the sake of humans' redemption. It is on this basis that Anselm proves the necessity of Christ's death and thus raises to understanding the rationality of God's action in creation and redemption.[84] On the other hand, we may ask of Barth whether his criticisms of Anselm's presentation do not reveal a tendency in his theological method of raising to understanding the particularity of the humanity of Jesus' life act through its direct association with the inconceivable act in which God posits God's self, that is, to convert the contingency and relativity of creaturely being into an aspect of an all encompassing idea. It is not clear how Barth might avoid this possibility.

---

82. K Barth, *Church Dogmatics* 4/1 (Edinburgh: T&T Clark, 1956), 486.
83. Anselm, *op cit*, Book 1, ch xii, 205f.
84. McIntyre, *op cit*, 184, 190.

The *Filioque*—An Opportunity for Debate?

The current discussion of the proposal from the World Council of Churches that 'all churches should revert to the original text of the Nicene Creed as the normative formulation' and thus excise the *filioque*, presents churches with a unique opportunity for extensive re-examination of fundamental theology.[1]

One of the difficulties presented by such a proposal is that both East and West have deeply engrained in their cultural psyche unexamined assumptions about each other's way of doing theology.

> The difference between the two conceptions (East and West) of the Trinity determines the whole character of theological thought . . . the difference is such that it becomes difficult to apply the same name of theology to the two different ways of dealing with divine realities.[2]

From a quite different perspective—dealing with the Eastern church's attitude to the *filioque*, no less a theologian than Karl Barth expresses his incomprehension that Eastern theologians can find the *filioque* responsible for such doctrines as the immaculate conception and papal infallibility. On the other hand the East's rejection of the *filioque* must be understood as tantamount to tri-theism![3]

---

1. *Spirit of God, Spirit of Christ—Ecumenical Reflections on the Filioque Controversy*, L Vischer ed, (London: SPCK, 1981), vi.

2. V Lossky, *In the Image and Likeness of God* (London: Mowbrays, 1974), 80.

3. K Barth, *Church Dogmatics* 1/1 (Edinburgh: T&T Clark, 1936), 551ff.

If we as Westerners are to come to terms with the issues raised by the Eastern church regarding the addition of the *filioque* to the text of the Nicene-Constantinopolitan creed, there are certain basic aspects of their approach which need to be appreciated.

I take as a starting point the observation made by Karl Rahner that in Western theology the doctrine of the one God, as distinct from the Trinity, assumed primary importance. The Trinity in the West became locked into splendid isolation. We speak, he says,

> of the necessary metaphysical properties of God, but not of God as experienced in salvation history in his free relations to his creatures. For should one make use of salvation history, it would soon become apparent that one speaks of him whom scripture and Jesus calls Father, Jesus' Father, who sends the Son and who gives himself to us in the Spirit.[4]

What Rahner draws attention to has deep roots in the history of dogma in the West and the East. This may be indicated by way of illustration from that history. If we look at St Basil the Great's defence of the deity of the Holy Spirit in his work *De Spiritu Sancto*,[5] we are immediately struck by the fact that his argument has a definite form and structure which follows his understanding of the purpose and content of the divine liturgy.[6] It is certainly not without significance, if we are to

---

4. K Rahner, *The Trinity* (London: Burns and Oates, 1970), 18

5. Basil, *'De Spiritu Sancto'*, *The Library of Nicene and Post-Nicene Fathers*, vol viii, P Schaff and H Wace eds, (Grand Rapids: Eerdmans, 1984).

6. It is unfortunate that K Rahner, *op cit*, 18, note 13, proceeds to categorise Greek thought as 'formalistic' without seeking the basis of the Greek reluctance to inquire about hypostatic relations in God within the doxological context of liturgical language in which the dogma of the Trinity is rooted.

grasp St Basil's intentions, that he indicates the liturgical context of the dispute.[7]

Those who questioned the deity of the Spirit maintained that, since the preposition 'in' the liturgical phrase 'in the Spirit' predicated creaturely circumscription of that which by nature is uncircumscribed, the Spirit cannot be said to be equal with the Father. The latter is implied by the preposition 'with' the ascriptions embedded in the liturgy.[8] Basil replies that his opponents have failed to take account in their thinking of the primary distinction, presupposed by liturgy, between God's essential and incomprehensible unity, his *ousia*, and the hypostatic economy of the history of salvation.[9] The former cannot be thought of as divided or circumscribed in any sense; consequently his opponents protest correctly against any division which could introduce polytheism into the church.[10] God's essential being, God's undivided unity remains; but Basil does not deny that such words as 'of', 'through' and 'in' are properly predicated of God. The church recognises both aspects: the ineffable, undivided *ousia* of God, and the hypostatic economy expressed in words which imply local movement. Here we note two things which are of permanent importance in St Basil's argument and in appreciating Greek theological method.

1. God's relationship with the world is understood in terms of the specific historical content of the history of salvation in which the trinitarian *hypostases* are active for the creation and reconciliation of the world.

2. The relationship between the *hypostases* and the unity of God is understood in terms of an ineffability which, celebrated in the doxological ascriptions of the liturgy, is directly proportional to the voluntary nature of God's

---

7.   Basil, *op cit*, sec 1 3.
8.   *Ibid*, sec 4 6.
9.   *Ibid*, sec 5 7.
10.   *Ibid*, secs 5 & 6.

condescension to the creature in its relative, created, contingency.

The theological importance for St Basil of this distinction between the trinitarian *hypostases* and the ineffable unity of God's essential being cannot be over-emphasised. It derives directly from and gives expression to the liturgical celebration of the creature's ontological renewal by God's free action in history. Therefore to predicate prepositions applicable to the economy of salvation, eg 'through' and 'in', of God's ineffable essence is to call into question the very basis of the church's life. It questions the free nature of God's condescension and makes thereby the reason for the church's doxology a cause for dividing God's unity. For the economy did not take place that God's being might be added to, but that the creature as a creature may be renewed.[11] This method gives rise to highly paradoxical language. Basil speaks of the Spirit as

> impassibly divided, shared without loss or ceasing to be entire . . . to everyone who receives it, as though given to him alone, and yet it sends forth grace sufficient and full for all mankind.[12]

This language is a direct result of the basically liturgical structure of St Basil's argument in which statements are made which refer to God in quite distinct and logically incompatible ways.

There are those statements which refer to God's ineffable and undivided unity. This is the sense in which 'with' is ascribed to the Spirit—'with the Father and the Son'. These statements are concerned with God who is distinct from his activity, who performs his deeds of creation and redemption with a freedom which corresponds to the ineffability of his

---

11. Basil, *op cit*, sec 8 18: 'Shall his care for us degrade to meanness our thoughts of Him?'
12. Basil, *op cit*, sec 9 22.

nature, and are doxological in form.[13] That is to say, they are statements in which

> the otherwise usual sense of the word is surrendered
> in its being used to praise God—the word is released
> from the manipulation of our thought and we must
> learn ever anew from the reality of God what the
> word properly means.[14]

On the other hand there are those sorts of statements which serve as the basis of the church's doxological ascriptions: these fall into the category of what St Basil calls *kerygma* and refer to the fixed tradition concerning the economy of salvation.[15] The structural differences between these two sorts of statements are not amenable to logical correlation of the one with the other. This is precisely what St Basil's opponents attempted to do. The history of Jesus is the subject of didactic tradition and witness; Jesus Christ, true God and true man, is the subject of doxological ascription. We cannot adduce or give theoretical explanations of the historical events of Christ's humiliation and exaltation from the confession 'very God and very man'. Serious logical problems, which soon become theological problems, arise once these statements are abstracted from the *Sitz im Leben* of the doxological structure of the liturgy.

To prevent this confusion, to which his opponents had succumbed, Basil enjoins, 'Dogma is to be observed in silence',

---

13. This question and the legitimacy of such statements is argued in the debate between H Gollwitzer, *The Existence of God* (London: SCM, 1965) and E Jüngel, *The Doctrine of the Trinity* (Edinburgh: Scottish Academic Press, 1976).
14. W Pannenberg, *Basic Questions in Theology*, vol 1 (London: SCM, 1970), 216.
15. Basil, *op cit*, sec 2 and 3 4 5. See also E Schlink, *The Coming Christ and the Coming Church* (Edinburgh: Oliver and Boyd, 1970), 16ff, 87ff.

and 'the meaning of dogma is difficult of understanding for the very advantage of the reader'.[16]

We note then in Basil's argument a direct relationship between a correct understanding of theological reflection and what is celebrated in and presupposed by the liturgy. To impugn the Spirit's deity, to dispute the doxological ascription 'with' as implying the Spirit's ineffable unity with the Father and the Son, is to call into question the historical content of the hypostatic economy of the Son which is made possible by the Spirit. It is thus also to deny the ontological renewal of the creature celebrated in the liturgy.

In order to bring these considerations to bear on the basic problem of understanding between Eastern and Western theological method we now turn to consider how representative Western theologians deal with the issues which Basil himself addressed.

The Trinity in Western Thought

When we look at Tertullian's use of the idea of economy as a means of understanding the Trinity in relation to creation and its redemption, it is notable that for him the economy is a means of explaining the eternal intra-trinitarian relationships in such a way that, on the principle that division of authority does not imply division of essence, it can be affirmed that God is both one in three and three in one.[17] He then uses the illustration of human thought and consciousness to show that the trinitarian

---

16. Basil, *op cit*, sec 27 76. Cf D Bonhoeffer, *Christology* (London: Collins, 1966): 'To speak of Christ means to keep silent; to be silent is to speak. The proclamation of Christ is the church speaking from a proper silence . . . We must study Christ in the humble silence of the worshipping community' (27).

17. Tertullian, *Adv Praxean, Ante Nicene Christian Library*, vol xv, no 11 (Edinburgh: T&T Clark, 1970), ch 3.

mode of being is not a threat to God's unity.[18] In the hands of St Augustine this kind of analogy was to assume great importance in Western trinitarian thought.

For Tertullian it is this analogy and the logic of the implied relationships between unity and difference, rather than the historical particularity of the content of the history of salvation, which serves as the basis for understanding the distinctness of the trinitarian hypostases.[19]

The idea of unity expressed by Tertullian has been aptly described as 'organic'[20] in that the unity of God is established by an organising principle which administers its authority in a threefold manner. In confirmation of this interpretation we note what Harnack has drawn to our attention, namely the link between Tertullian's understanding of the economy and his Montanism.[21] On the basis of his understanding of God's unity Tertullian proposes a structural analogy between the essence of God and the history of the world whereby the dispensations of the Father and the Son are followed by the Spirit. World history is here structured according to the nature of deity in a manner which would be unthinkable for St Basil. For the East the economy takes place for the renewal of the creature, not that God's essence may be revealed. To adopt such a structural analogy as proposed by Tertullian is to do precisely what was later achieved by the addition of the *filioque*. The hypostatic origin of the Spirit is sought in terms of an intra-trinitarian relationship as distinct from the view which understands the hypostasis of the Spirit in terms which give expression to the ineffable unity of God and the hypostatic economy.[22]

---

18. Tertullian, *op cit*, ch 5; cf A Harnack, *History of Dogma*, vol II (London: Williams and Norgate, 1897), 257ff.

19. *Ibid*, ch 7.

20. G Prestige, *God in Patristic Thought* (London: SPCK, 1956), 97.

21. A Harnack, *op cit*, 262ff.

22. See A I C Heron, *The Holy Spirit in the Bible, the History of Christian Thought and Recent Theology* (Westminster Press, 1983), 176f.

We therefore find that already in Tertullian significant differences emerge as to the nature and function of the trinitarian economy when compared with the Eastern church, differences which will later assume critical importance in the definition of dogma. This difference is primarily due to the different roles played in trinitarian dogma by the historical content of salvation history. In the West the question of the unity of God and its relation to the world's reconciliation and redemption is seen in terms of analogies which emphasise the unity of world history and the being of God. This understanding will give rise to the problem of how the difference between Creator and creature can be maintained without deifying the creature or dividing the Godhead.

The same sorts of questions arise in the Western development of trinitarian thought on through St Augustine. Commenting on the use by the Greeks of the words *hypostaseis* and *ousia*, a distinction which was critical for St Basil's argument in defence of the Spirit's deity, he says:

> They (the Greeks) intend to put a difference, I know not what, between *ousia* and *hypostasis*, so that most of ourselves who treat these things in the Greek language are accustomed to saying *mian ousian, treis hypostasis*, or in Latin one essence, three substances. But because with us the usage already obtained, that by essence we understand the same thing which is understood by substance we do not say one essence three substances, but one essence or substance and three persons in that we could not find any more suitable way by which to enunciate in words that which we understand without them.[23]

We understand this statement to signify that the crucial difference between the ineffable essence of the one God and the hypostatic economy, which formed the basis for St Basil's

---

23. Augustine, *On the Trinity,* in *The Works of St Augustine* (Edinburgh: T&T Clark, 1873), chs 8 and 9, secs 9-10.

distinction between kerygma and dogma, is ignored. It is on this distinction that he based his defence of the deity of the Spirit in the context of the divine liturgy. For St Augustine it means, 'I know not what!'

Augustine introduces the word 'person' because substance can too easily be confused with essence. Far from being related to the particularity of the historical content of the economy of salvation, person is introduced as a terminological variable to signify a distinction which is understood without words. It is not the closeness of meaning which exists between substance and essence that is altered by the word person, but rather their unity of meaning whilst avoiding the charge of tritheism. It is therefore a logical device necessitated by the exigencies of the Latin language rather than the reality of the distinction annunciated by the historical content of the economy.[24]

The *Filioque* and Western Tradition

The provenance of the *filioque* in Western theological thought derives from an attempt to defend the deity of the Spirit by seeking its hypostatic origin in a relationship between the Father and the Son. The development of trinitarian thought in the West until the formal consolidation of the *filioque* in creedal formulation shows the clear influence of the line from Tertullian and Augustine. The major Western steps in this process are relatively well known.[25]

The twentieth century has witnessed a renewed interest in trinitarian thought in the West consequent on Karl Barth's monumental attempt to make the dogma of the Trinity the basic

---

24. See V Lossky, *The Mystical Theology of the Eastern Church* (Cambridge: J Clarke, 1957), 85ff, and T F Torrance, *Theological Science* (London: Oxford University Press), 189ff.
25. D Ritschl, 'Historical Developments and Implications of the Filioque Controversy', in L Vischer, *op cit*, 48ff.

methodological principle for theology.[26] However, as will become apparent, the development of the dogma of the Trinity in Barth's dogmatics serves to re-emphasise the prevailing Western tendency to seek the hypostatic origin of the Spirit *ab utroque*, and thus to base hypostatic diversity on the principle of juxtaposed relations rather than on distinctions grounded in the historical content of the economy.

Karl Barth's Defence of the *Filioque*

As Barth sees it his defence of the *filioque* is

> no less than the entire statement of our view . . . of the doctrine of the Holy Spirit and the Trinity in general.[27]

The *filioque* is an expression of the means and confirmation of the way Barth achieves understanding of the historical content of revelation. On this basis

> we are completely tied to the rule—and regard this as fundamental—that pronouncements upon the reality, of the divine modes of existence, 'antecedently in themselves' could not in content be any different from those that have to be made about their reality in revelation.[28]

The *filioque* 'proves', ie brings to understanding, the event of revelation as presupposing the inconceivable event in which God posits Godself as Lord. The subjective reality and possibility of knowledge of God is in the Spirit in whom God affirms Godself as both One and Another in the freedom of love.

---

26. K Barth, *Church Dogmatics*, 1/1 (Edinburgh: T&T Clark, 1936), secs. 4-8. See also G Watson, 'Karl Barth and St Anselm's Theological Program', *Scottish Journal of Theology* 30: 31-45 (included in this volume).
27. K Barth, *Church Dogmatics* 1/1 (Edinburgh: T&T Clark, 1936), 556.
28. *Ibid.*

> The phrase (ie the *filioque*) is in the first place the
> description of the divinity of the Holy Spirit, in this
> case not in respect of the *opus ad extra* common to the
> three modes of existence, but in respect of its reality
> as a divine mode of existence, ie of its reality in
> relation to the other divine modes of existence.[29]

Barth rejects any suggestion that instead of the *filioque* one could substitute the modified form of 'from the Father *through* the Son'. He maintains that this modified interpretation disputes the *relatio originis* between the Son and the Spirit, so that the Spirit can only 'improperly' be called the Spirit of the Son. Further, the unity of God is called into question by this modified form. It presupposes that, in relation to the Spirit, Father and Son do not have all things in common. Instead of the Father being the Father of the Son and so by implication, per the *filioque*, the origin of the Spirit with the Son, the origin of the Spirit is postulated as a second function alongside God's Fatherhood.[30]

Barth further insists that the *filioque* has a positive intent as distinct from its negative implications regarding the way in which the church should describe the possibility of creaturely knowledge of God in God's self revelation. The *filioque* celebrates the extent to which God is free in Godself for relationships with that which is distinct from God.

> By being the Father who brings forth the Son, He
> brings forth the Spirit of love; for by bringing forth
> the Son, God already negates in himself, from all
> eternity, in his utter simplicity, existence in loneliness
> . . . God is directed towards the Other, will only
> possess himself by possessing himself along with the
> Other, in fact in the Other.[31]

---

29.   *Ibid*, 542.
30.   *Ibid*, 552.
31.   *Ibid*, 553.

This means that the *filioque* is that which in God presupposes the possibility of God being the Creator of that which is distinct from Godself. As The Spirit of the Father and the Son, the Spirit is that which negates God's 'existence in loneliness'; the Spirit is the Spirit of God's love. Hence,

> In the Son of his love, ie in the Son in and with whom he brings himself forth as love, He then brings forth also in the *opus ad extra*, in creation, the creaturely reality distinct from Himself, and in revelation, reconciliation and peace for the creature that has fallen away from him . . . He is love antecedently in Himself as the Father of the Son. That is the interpretation and proof of the *qui procedit a Patre*.[32]

Since it is through the Son of God, by whose bringing forth God negates in Godself existence in loneliness, and since as God the Son of God could not be less the origin of the love which negates this loneliness, it must further be asked:

> If revelation would not be revelation without the outpouring and impartation of the Spirit, by which man becomes God's child, should not the Spirit be directly the Spirit of the Son as well? But if so . . . how can He be so, if He is not in reality, in the reality of God antecedently in Himself? . . . In this way we interpret and prove the *qui procedit ex Patre Filioque*.[33]

The Question of *Spirituque*?

Barth raises the question

> whether, to correspond with the procession of the Spirit from the Father and the Son, there ought also to be asserted a procession of the Son from the Father and the Spirit.[34]

---

32. *Ibid*, 553.
33. *Ibid*, 554.
34. *Ibid*.

Barth admits certain exegetical considerations in support of this view and also a certain systematic argument in its defence. The systematic argument runs:

> If we apply our rule here also, that dogmatic pronouncements upon the immanent Trinity can and must be read off according to content from the determinations about God's modes of existence in revelation, are we not in that case forced to assume also between the Spirit and the Son an original relationship, which in that case would be neither generation nor breathing but a third thing? . . . that only then is the circle of mutual relations, in which God is One in Three modes of existence, a complete and self enclosed one, and that already for that reason such an origin of the Son from the Father and the Spirit is to be postulated.[35]

Barth dismisses the argument on the grounds that if it were to succeed one would also have to postulate an origin of the Father from the Son and the Spirit. But, he contends, the mutual relations of the intra-trinitarian being of God are not such as to involve origins as such, but modes of existence of the one God. The systematic argument may be allowed in the sense that it is

> A further description of the *homoousia* of the Father, Son and Spirit, but with begetting and breathing it has

---

35. *Ibid*, 555. See also G Hendry, 'From the Father and the Son: The *Filioque* after 900 Years, *Theology Today* XI, 1954-55: 449; J McIntyre, The Holy Spirit in Greek Patristic Thought', *Scottish Journal of Theology* 7, 1954: 353ff, and 371-75. See also, the important discussion in T F Torrance, 'Trinity in Unity and Uniting in Trinity', in *The Christian Doctrine of God — One Being Three Persons* (Edinburgh: T&T Clark, 1996), ch 7, and in T F Torrance, 'Introduction', in *Reformed Orthodox Dialogue*, T F Torrance ed, (Edinburgh: T&T Clark, 1996), xviff.

nothing to do and so moreover does not require any completion in this direction.[36]

But the question arises with respect to this systematic argument: if the unity of God, of which Barth allows the argument to be 'a further description', is conceived in terms of the inconceivable freedom in which God posits Godself as God, and the historical content of revelation is only understood in terms of its presupposing this inconceivable decision, why should the argument only apply to modes of existence and not to origins? In principle, Barth cannot distinguish between modes of existence and the way in which God posits Godself as God. Barth. therefore uses a distinction which he realises is necessary, but he has excluded the only possible basis upon which it could be made, ie the historical relations of the hypostases in the economy of salvation.

This conclusion is confirmed when Barth applies his dogmatic method to the scriptural argument concerning a *Spirituque*. In describing the relation between the Spirit and the Son in the conception of Jesus by the Spirit Barth maintains:

> The incarnation of the Son of God out of Mary cannot indeed consist of the origination for the first time, here and now of the Son of God, but it consists in the Son of God taking to himself here and now, this other thing which exists in Mary, namely flesh . . . the dogma of the Virgin Birth by no means specifically claims that the Holy Spirit is the Father of the man Jesus and so, when the Son of God became man, becomes also the Father of the Son of God. But it claims that the man Jesus has no Father (exactly in the way in which as the Son of God He has no mother). What is ascribed to the Holy Spirit in the birth of Christ, is the assumption of humanness in the Virgin Mary into unity with God in the Logos mode of existence . . . This work of the Spirit is proto-typical of

---

36.   K Barth, *Church Dogmatics* 1/1 (Edinburgh: T&T Clark, 1936), 556.

> the work of the Spirit in the becoming of the children
> of God . . . But the work of the Spirit is not ectypical of
> a work of the Spirit upon the Son of God himself.[37]

This argument holds only if we assume with Barth that the Scriptures witness to the historical content of revelation only in the sense in which that content is to be understood in direct relationship with the ineffable essence, the inconceivable act, in which God posits Godself as God. But the Scriptures direct our attention to actual this-worldly events as the way in which God has condescended to humankind, not in order to reveal the realities and possibilities inherent in God's being the God that God is; but that the creature may be renewed as a creature.

This entails, in the case of the Virgin Birth, that for Barth, since the inconceivable act in which God posits Godself can never be the subject of the ontic distinctions involved in the scriptural witness to revelation, that these distinctions refer only to the humanity of Jesus and not to the Son of God.

We thus arrive at a position which has uncanny similarities with that adopted by Nestorius who maintained that since the Son of God did not derive his existence as God from Mary she could not be called *Theotokos*. As St Cyril never tired of pointing out, this means interpreting the 'made man' of the Nicene Symbol as 'man is made man'. It becomes a tautology and the incarnation is denied.[38] Barth sets out his defence of the *filioque* in terms of a defence of 'the entire statement of our view . . . of the Holy Spirit and of the Trinity in general',[39] and in the last resort is forced to use the device of separating the ontic content of the economy, Christ's birth, from the definition of his hypostasis on the basis that, after all, Mary is not the mother of a divine origin. This highlights both the artificiality of Barth's

---

37. *Ibid.*
38. Cyril, *Five Tomes Against the Blasphemies of Nestorius* (Oxford: Parker & Rivingtons, 1881), Tome 1, 28ff.
39. K Barth, *Church Dogmatics* 1 / 1 (Edinburgh: T&T Clark, 1936), 556.

methodology and the difficulty of justifying the *filioque* as a meaningful theological relationship in this context.

Conclusion

Karl Barth's exposition and defence of the *filioque* highlights the importance of the question of theological method in understanding both its function and meaning in the Western and Eastern theological traditions.[40]

The critical difference which bears on the discussion of the *filioque* is the function, in the respective Western and Eastern interpretations, of the distinction between God's ineffable and undivided unity and the economy of salvation in which the hypostases act in accord for the purpose of the renewal of the creature. The West has generally reflected a concern to express the divine unity rather than the particularity of the hypostases' differences in terms of their historical activity. This has systemically tended towards a modalism in which the distinctness of the hypostases has become blurred.[41] In the East, where there is a concern to emphasise the threefoldness and to see the hypostasis of the Father as the sole originator of the hypostatic difference of the Son and the Spirit, there is a tendency toward subordinationism and consequently tritheism,[42] a cutting off of the history of salvation from its primary source in God's unity.

However, what has generally been overlooked in this 'text book' type approach to the question of the difference between

---

40. See also J Pelikan, *A History of the Development of Doctrine*, vol 2 (University of Chicago, 1974), 190ff.
41. See K Rahner, *op cit*. Cf A I C Heron, 'Who Proceedeth from the Father and the Son; The Problem of the Filioque', *Scottish Journal of Theology* 24/2, 1971: 159ff; Heron, *The Holy Spirit, op cit*, 167, 172ff; J Moltmann, *The Trinity and the Kingdom of God* (London: SCM, 1981), 157ff.
42. Cf K Barth, *Church Dogmatics* 1/1 (Edinburgh: T&T Clark, 1936), 550-52; cf 450ff.

East and West, this balancing of weight to be given to differing strands of legitimate thought about the Trinity, is that the differences arise from the contexts in which the doctrine is understood.

As has been indicated, the liturgical and doxological setting of the doctrine in the East entails a distinction being made between the economy of salvation and the ineffable undivided essence or *ousia* of God. This distinction is not made primarily on logical or philosophical grounds, in order to preserve the idea of the non-necessity in God of God's movement toward the creature for its salvation.[43] The distinction gives expression to the experience of salvation celebrated in the liturgy.[44] For example, the mystery of the incarnation of the Son of God cannot be understood in terms of positive speculation about the nature of deity. Silence before this mystery, an attitude of adoration, becomes the means of communication and of understanding since the experience of union with God is the basis of knowledge of doctrine. Theology here 'is not the science of divine ontology, but of divine revelation'.[45]

God then is not known or worshipped according to his *ousia* or essence, which remains supremely unknowable, but on the basis of God's 'procession outwards'.[46] This is the economy of salvation in history, which takes place for the renovation and renewal of the creature, not for the sake of revealing the divine essence. The awful mystery, which is at the heart of the experience of union with God, celebrated in the liturgy, is directly proportional to the voluntary nature of the movement by which the economy of the *hypostases* proceeds forth from God. Its purpose is to lead our minds not to knowledge of concepts about God, but union with God. As such it raises our

---

43. Contra J Moltmann, *op cit*, 151. Cf H Gollwitzer, *The Existence of God Confessed by Faith* (London: SCM, 1965), 217.
44. Cf J Pelikan, *op cit*, 259 and 2ff.
45. *Ibid*, 33.
46. *Ibid*.

human being to realities which pass understanding, thus the dogmas of the church

> often present themselves to the human reason as antinomies, the more difficult to resolve the more sublime the mystery they express. It is not a question of suppressing the antinomy by adapting dogma to our understanding, but of a change of heart and mind enabling us to attain to the contemplation of reality which reveals itself to us as it raises us to God and unites us, according to our several capacities, with God.[47]

We would agree with the observation of D Ritschl, that consideration of the dogma of the Trinity and the *filioque* in particular must take into account this aspect of the Eastern church's approach to dogma. Thus any reference to the Trinity must be seen as

> originally doxological. That doxological affirmations are not primarily definitions or descriptions, rather (they are) ascriptive lines of thought, speech and action which are offered to God himself . . . (consequently attention needs to be given to) the actual experience of the early Christians to the synthetic thoughts, mostly in doxological dress, concerning God's presence in Israel, in the coming of Jesus and in the church.[48]

This basic characteristic of the structure of Eastern theological reflection has not been taken into account sufficiently in Western responses regarding the question of the *filioque*. It is true that Sabellianism, 'opened or concealed, implies that the trinitarian structure of redemption has nothing really to do with

---

47. V Lossky, *The Mystical Theology of the Eastern Church* (J Clarke, 1957), 42. Cf St Basil above, and E Schlink, *The Coming Christ and The Coming Church, op cit*, 58ff.

48. D Ritschl, 'Historical Development and Implications of the *Filioque* Controversy', 64f; and A I C Heron, *The Holy Spirit, op cit*, 173.

the nature of God, and loses hold on God in his own reality,[49] and that the Eastern doctrine is one in which 'a Spirit that proceeds in eternity from the Father alone would seem to stand in a different eternal relation to the Son from that enacted and realised in the movement from incarnation to Pentecost'.[50] But it would be premature to draw the conclusion that such implies the necessity to 'affirm a double relationship between the Son and the Spirit which is as ultimate in the life of God as in the work of salvation'.[51]

But the distinction made between the ineffable essence or *ousia* of God and the economy, God's ineffable unity and God's procession into the world, does not imply a division between the unity of divine being and action in and of itself and in the world; but draws attention to the fact that the grace, power and action of the economy, whilst nevertheless uncreated and eternal, does not involve the *ousia* or essence of God. As Photius pointed out,[52] whatever is common to two hypostases had to be common to all three, otherwise there would be division in the Godhead. Consequently if the unity revealed in the economy between the Father and the Son, in respect of the giving of the Holy Spirit, is also common to the Spirit then the Spirit is author of himself. Then all the distinctions and relationships, introduced by the *filioque* to protect the structure of redemption as grounded in God's being as such, turn out to commit the Sabellian error! For if the unity of the divine action is grounded in all three hypostases there remains no basis for insisting which particular hypostases is incarnate or sent.

It may be objected[53] that it is 'as Father of the Son not as monarch of the Godhead that the Father in eternity breathes the

---

49. A Heron, *op cit*, 173.
50. A Heron, *op cit*, 177.
51. *Ibid*.
52. J Pelikan, *op cit*, 194.
53. See on the following: J Moltmann, 'Theological Perspectives Towards the Resolution of the Filioque Controversy', in E Vischer,

Spirit', so that the Spirit is an expression of the relationship between the Father and the Son, without making this hypostasis the ground of that relationship, for that ground is the Fatherhood of the Father.[54] In that case it needs to be seen that this renewed interpretation of the *filioque* 'no longer coincides properly speaking with the *filioque*, for it affirms a distinction between the Father and the Son in what they give to the Spirit, while the *filioque* confounds the Father and the Son in the common impersonal substance'.[55]

It is precisely this distinction that is safeguarded by the liturgical structure of the East's approach to the trinitarian dogma.[56] The Father is Father as the origin of the hypostasis of the Spirit not according to the common essence shared with the Son and the Spirit, but in that by which the Father is distinguished from them as Father of the Son and Spirator of the Spirit. This entails that the Father is such an origin, 'not according to his nature or essence (which was common to all three hypostases), but according to his hypostasis as Father'.[57] While this distinction is 'built into' the East's approach to

---

op cit, 164ff and J Moltmann, *The Trinity and the Kingdom of God*, op cit, 182ff; A Heron, 'Who Proceedeth from the Father and the Son ...', 161ff; A Heron, *The Holy Spirit*, op cit, 166ff; V Lossky, *The Image and Likeness of God*, op cit, 81ff.

54. J Moltmann, *op cit*, 172; A Heron, Who Proceedeth from the Father and the Son ...', *op cit*, 164ff; and A Heron, *The Holy Spirit*, op cit, 177f.

55. D Staniloae, 'The Procession of the Holy Spirit from the Father and His Relation to the Son', in Vischer, *op cit*, 177. See 176 quoting St Gregory Palamas: 'The Spirit has his existence from The Father of the Son because he who causes the Spirit to proceed is also the Father'. Cf A Heron, 'Who Proceedeth from the Father and the Son ...', 164-66, and A Heron, *The Holy Spirit*, op cit, 177-78; J Moltmann, *op cit*, 182ff.

56. T Stylianopoulos, 'The Filioque: Dogma, Theologumenon or Error?' *Greek Orthodox Theological Review* 31, 1986: 258ff.

57. J Pelikan, *op cit*, 197.

dogma as an expression of the reality of the creature's union with God celebrated in the liturgy as a consequence of God's going forth from Godself for the sake of the creature, it is difficult to see how this distinction can be maintained in the West. For example, it is held[58] that while Moltmann recognises the implied modalism of the *filioque*,[59] his emphasis on the historical distance between the Father and the Son in relation to the Spirit presupposes the dereliction of the Son and the eschatological fulfillment of God's purpose in history by the Spirit, provides grounds for obviating this difficulty. But it is difficult to see how this might be so. For if the distinctions observed in the economy of salvation are the distinctions involved in God's being in becoming who God is in relation to the world, since Moltmann rejects any distinction between the immanent and economic Trinity on the basis of an analysis of the concept of love,[60] it is difficult to see how this procedure can avoid the errors reminiscent of Marcellus of Ancyra.[61]

What is at stake here is not whether God's being and God's actions are expressions of the self-same love,[62] but whether the common action of the hypostases in the economy, which takes place for the sake of the renewal of the creature qua creature and not that the ineffable essence of God might be revealed, is that by which both the unity and the distinctions in trinitarian doctrine are grounded and maintained. We would contend that the attempt to read the economy back into God's *ousia*, however carefully the distinctions are maintained, inevitably tends toward some form of modalism wherein either the godhead is divided or the creature is divinised.

---

58. A Heron, *The Holy Spirit, op cit*, 169f.
59. J Moltmann, *The Trinity and the Kingdom of God*, 136ff, 167.
60. J Moltmann, *op cit*, 151. The two (immanent and economic) 'rather form a continuity and merge into one another' (152).
61. J Pelikan, *op cit*, 193.
62. J Moltmann, *op cit*, 151f; cf A Heron, *The Holy Spirit, op cit*, 177f.

Part Two

The Church, Its Marks and Mission

Reformed Ecclesiology in the Context of *Koinonia*: the Nature of the Church, its Unity and Mission

The paper's rather grandiose title is an attempt to limit the scope of its content, 'a Reformed ecclesiology', by relating it to the use of the term *koinonia* in ecumenical discussion about the nature of the church.

When one considers the popular image of the Reformers, they seem to be better remembered for their mistakes rather than their achievements. The scandal of Luther's completely unjustifiable anti-Jewish outburst, the ambiguities of his stance in the Peasants Revolt, and his misguided sanction of the bigamy of Philip of Hesse, have created the picture of a powerful though thoroughly inconsistent personality given to swings of mood and temper that is difficult to reconcile with the claims of fundamental theological insight and profound piety attributed to him.

Calvin's popular image could hardly be said to be more sympathetic. If Luther appears prone to inconsistency, Calvin seems almost too consistent. His attempts at establishing authentic Christian community, characterised by doctrinal soundness and moral integrity, appear like efforts to create an ecclesiastical police state.

In view of these popular images it does not seem surprising that the general impact of the Reformation on the life and thought of the churches today is not very noticeable. Yet when one considers to what extent the Reformation shaped the theology and the institutional structures of the churches in the West, both Protestant and Catholic, this forgetfulness seems problematic. This appears to be the case also in ecumenical circles. The Reformers' conception of the church seems to be treated either as a historic monument of purely historical interest or a doctrinal *shibboleth* which introduces an unpleasant note of divisiveness into the amiable atmosphere of ecumenical dialogue. But it is also the case in those churches which owe their identity to being established on the basis of the Reformers' ecclesiology. Very often the main features of the teaching of the Reformers is buried in these communions under the complicated and contentious history of interpretation.

An exposition of the main features of a Reformed ecclesiology is offered in what follows in the hope that both Reformed and Catholic partners in ecumenical encounter can profit from an increased awareness of the basic orientation of a Reformed view of the church. At least we may expect such an exercise to provide a basis for assessing how far the original conflict between the Reformers and the late medieval Roman church is still present, and to what extent the issues at stake have changed over time. It may not be helpful in generating unqualified ecumenical enthusiasm, but I believe it could help to increase the clarity of our theological perceptions and the realism of our ecumenical expectations.

The famous statement with which Calvin begins his *Institutes,* that 'true and solid wisdom, consists almost entirely of two parts: the knowledge of God and of ourselves',[1] is shown in the rest of that work to be grounded on his understanding of the incarnation. The *Institutes* are structured according to the trinitarian structure of the Apostle's Creed. The central core of Calvin's exposition is in Books 2 and 3, dealing with Christ and the Spirit. At the conclusion of Book 2 he sums up his exposition by indicating that 'we see all parts of salvation are comprehended in Christ (Acts 4 v 12). We should take care therefore not to derive the least portion of it from anywhere else'.[2] Not only does Calvin here stress the fact that Christ took to himself the consequences of our sin, 'if acquittal in his condemnation, . . . if reconciliation in his descent into hell'. He

---

1. J Calvin, *Institutes of the Christian Religion* (Grand Rapids: Eerdmans, reprinted 1975), Book 1 1 37.
2. Calvin, *op cit*, Book 2, 16 9.

also equally stressed the fact of Christ's active obedience on our behalf, as one united with us in his humanity. Christ is our righteousness, and since such 'rich store of every kind of merit abounds in him, let us drink our fill from this fountain and no other'.[3]

This line of thought is developed by Calvin in regard to his understanding of the church's worship. Christ in his risen humanity is our High Priest. He offered the sacrifice of his own body. He intercedes for his church as both priest and victim. The common bond of our humanity which he assumed means that, 'although in ourselves polluted, we are priests in Him'.[4] Just as the Jewish high priest entered the holy of holies with the names of the twelve tribes engraved on stones upon his shoulders, 'so in the person of the one man all entered the sanctuary together, for our High Priest has entered heaven not only for Himself but for us'.[5]

This leads Calvin on to the central thrust of Book 3 where he insists that all that Christ did for us would be of no avail unless the Holy Spirit unites us to Him.[6] The work of the Spirit creates faith in us by means of the Word and sacraments which Christ has instituted in the church as the means of its union with himself. In this teaching Calvin insisted there was nothing new. When challenged by Cardinal Sadolet he defended his support of the reform of the church by saying, 'All we have attempted has been to renew the ancient face of the church'.[7] Calvin understood this renewal to consist in recovering the centrality of the person and work of Christ present to the church in the sanctifying power of the Holy Spirit in Word and sacrament.

---

3.   *Ibid.*
4.   Book 2, 15 6.
5.   *Ibid.* Cf J Calvin, *Commentary on Hebrews* (London: J Clarke, 1965), 6 19.
6.   *Institutes*, Book 3, 1 1.
7.   J Calvin, 'Letter to Sadolet', *Library of Christian Classics*, vol 22 (Philadelphia: Westminster Press, 1954), 231ff.

Whereas Cardinal Sadolet defined the church as that Body which always and everywhere had been directed by the Spirit of Christ, Calvin replied:

> What becomes of the Word of the Lord, the clearest of all marks, which the Lord himself in designating the church so often commends to us? For seeing how dangerous it would be to boast of the Spirit without the Word, Christ declared that the church is indeed governed by the Holy Spirit, but in order that this government might not be vague and unstable he bound it to the Word of God. For this reason Christ exclaims that those who are of God hear the Word of God, for his sheep are those who recognise the voice of their Shepherd . . . For this reason the Spirit by the mouth of Paul declares that the Church is built upon the foundation of the apostles and prophets.[8]

For Calvin the essential marks of the church are the preaching of the Word and the administration of the sacraments; these alone reveal the saving work of Christ completely. Bucer and Knox added discipline as a third mark of the church. Calvin admitted that discipline was very helpful but, nevertheless, 'When the preaching of the Gospel is reverently heard and the sacraments are not neglected, there the face of the church appears without deception or ambiguity'. Following closely St Paul's thought in Ephesians 4, Calvin sees the ministry of the church as God's gift to build up the church till it reaches a unity of faith, 'unto the measure of the stature of the fullness of Christ'.[9] To achieve this end certain functions need to be performed. The essential one is the proclamation of the Word and the administration of the sacraments. By this means Christ rules in his church by his grace. Calvin is quite flexible about the form this ministry might take, provided the functions of preaching and administration of the sacraments are fulfilled.

---

8.   *Ibid.*
9.   J Calvin, *Institutes of the Christian Religion*, Book 4, 3 5.

Calvin wrote to the King of Poland allowing not only bishops but an archbishop, as long as the abuses of the system then present were not followed.[10] In Geneva Calvin developed a fourfold order of ministry: pastors, teachers, elders and deacons.[11]

The church, then, in Calvin's view is grounded in God's purpose of reconciliation in Christ whereby humankind is called into fellowship with God and each other in him. Although Christ no longer lives on this earth he rules by his Word. The very fact that Christ has set up his rule in the church is proof 'that He is concerned about our salvation. Yes, He has borne witness that He will remain with His own and guide them to the end; and He continues to be objectively present through His ministers'.[12] As God clothed himself with our flesh in drawing near to the world in the incarnation of the Son of God, so God also continues to use earthly means in order to approach humankind. God offers God's self in earthen vessels.[13] God wills to speak to the world through human mouths and through visible elements—water, bread and wine. The church is the means by which the exalted Christ accomplishes his work among people.

Calvin sees the church as a mystery divinely established to serve the purpose of humankind's reconciliation. He therefore headed the decisive first chapter of his section on the church in his *Institutes*, 'Of the true church, with which we strive to be at one, since it is the mother of all the pious'.[14] Calvin characterises the church as 'mother' since he sees this as a metaphor received from the tradition of the church and one that is eminently appropriate since the church

---

10. *Letters of John Calvin*, J Bonner ed, vol 3 (Philadelphia, 1858), 111.
11. J Calvin, 'Draft Ecclesiastical Ordinances 1541', in *Library of Christian Classics, op cit*, 58.
12. *Corpus Reformatum* 50, 235.
13. J Calvin, *Institutes*, Book 4, 1 5.
14. *Ibid*, Book 4, 1 4.

receives and bears us in its womb, feeds us at its breasts, and then preserves us under its guardianship and guidance until we have put off this mortal flesh and have become like the angels. For our weakness does not permit that we should be dismissed from this school until we have spent our whole life there-in . . . Outside of its bosom there is no hope either of forgiveness of sins or any other felicity . . . Separation from the church always spells destruction.[15]

So Calvin repeats the early church dictum. *extra ecclesiam nulla salus*, 'outside the church there is no salvation'.

The reason why Calvin is so insistent on the necessity of the church as the sphere of God's redemptive activity is that it is to the church that Christ has promised the realisation of his presence in the Word and the sacraments. With such a view of the church Calvin says God lays upon us a 'yoke of humility'.[16] That is to say, we must surrender all our so-called personal and pious points of contact with God and humble ourselves before the Word of God which comes to us from another human being in whom we find the promise of eternal life. In this way 'God searchingly tests our obedience when we hear His servants not otherwise than if He Himself were speaking'.[17]

But these external signs to which Christ has so exclusively attached his promised presence, the church and its ministry of Word and sacraments, this seeming exclusivity is at one and the same time a merciful action in God's economy of salvation. God mercifully draws near to us in Christ through the church and its ministry, these human external means of preaching and the sacraments, for if God were to approach us directly we would be terrified by and swallowed up in God's awful presence. Through the church there is an accommodation by God to our situation, since 'we are so ignorant, slothful, and vain that we

---

15. *Ibid.*
16. *Ibid,* 4, 1 6.
17. *Ibid,* Book 4, 1 5.

need these external helps to allow faith to be born in us and grow unceasingly to its appointed end'.[18] This accommodation of God to our weakness and perversion, providing for us the church with its ministry of Word and sacraments, is similar to that accommodation in which God drew near to us in the incarnation of the Son of God.

Calvin also describes the church in terms of the New Testament metaphors of the Body of Christ and the congregation of the 'called' or 'elect'. In connection with this latter description he speaks of the church as also being invisible. After all that has previously been said about Calvin's doctrine of the church this cannot mean that he intends to weaken the connection of Christians with the church in whose bosom they are nurtured. Calvin's use of Augustine's distinction between the visible and invisible church is not meant to withdraw the visible church partly or wholly from the rule of Christ through His Word and sacraments. This distinctions means, in the first place, that we do not see the church in its totality, for to it belong people who have gone before us, as others will also come after us. Further, Calvin means that not all whom we now see to be members of the church belong to it in reality. Much chaff is mixed with the wheat.[19] But, and this is important in understanding the place of what later came to be called, for example in the Scots Confession, 'godly discipline' as a mark of the true church, Calvin does not lapse into idle speculation about who is in and who is out of the church's membership. The idea of a visible and invisible church emphasises the truth that we are Christians by grace alone and not by who or what we may think ourselves to be apart from God's Word of grace. It is in this context that Calvin discusses 'the true and false church'.[20]

---

18. *Ibid*, Book 4, 1 1.
19. *Ibid*, Book 4, 1 2 7.
20. *Ibid*, Book 4, 2.

The true church, in so far as it is an empirical reality, is visible to everyone. The same was true of the church's Lord when he lived on earth. But just as humankind in its enmity against God did not allow that Jesus was his Son, the church is no more recognisable as the Body of Christ in terms of its visible life. But, as has already been noted, Jesus Christ comes face to face with his people in the Word that is preached and the sacraments to which are attached Christ's promise of his presence. Calvin, with Melanchthon and the Lutheran Augsburg Confession of 1530, specified the marks of the true church as the pure preaching of the gospel and the right administration of the sacraments. 'In the preaching of Jesus Christ the countenance of God shines forth upon us. Where these signs, chosen by Christ Himself, appear in the visible world we can be certain that there Christ and his flock are to be found.'[21]

Calvin maintains that we cannot deduce from an assembly of pious people, in terms of its size or the ancient nature of its traditions, that such a body is the church. Against all fanatics he also holds that it is dangerous to refuse to believe in any church which does not evince perfect purity of life. He rejects as a demonic delusion the ideal of a spotless church.[22] The church for Calvin is defined by the proper use of the means Christ has chosen to create and maintain his church. That Calvin accepts only the Word and the sacraments as valid signs of the true church indicates that his doctrine of the church is a testimony to what he understands to be the sole lordship of Christ in the church.

This raises the question of schism and what Calvin understood to be the grounds for his sharp break with the church of Rome.[23] Calvin issued the most serious warnings against secession from the church for some doctrinal reason or

---

21. *Ibid*, Book 4, 1 9.
22. *Ibid*, Book 4, 1 13.
23. *Ibid*, Book 4, 2 5.

other. This is consistent with his view that whoever abandons the church, his mother, without sufficient cause, denies God and his Christ.[24] Christ's Body must not be torn asunder. Those who write about Calvin as if he was one who encouraged centrifugal forces in the church show that they have not actually read him. When he was expelled by the town council from Geneva, his followers refused to take part in the holy communion celebrated by pastors who were hostile to him. Calvin implored his friends to desist from their behaviour so that the unity of the church might not suffer harm. There is no reason to leave the church because its preaching contains some false elements and strange doctrines. 'For there is probably no church which is not marred by some degree of ignorance.'[25] Schism can be contemplated only when the message of salvation is no longer heard and the sacraments are perverted or set aside. Then Christ is no longer preached, and his church no longer exits in such circumstances. Calvin believed this to be the only possible reason for secession. He attempted to specify the fundamental points of doctrine which the church must unconditionally hold to qualify as church. Such an enumeration Calvin realised must always remain inadequate and provisional. But in the last resort what must never be impaired is the church's testimony to Jesus Christ, based on the prophetic and apostolic witness. Once that foundation is abandoned then the church ceases to qualify as church.[26]

The Question of *Koinonia* as a Means of Expressing the Nature of the Church, its Unity and Mission

The work of the World Council of Churches and, in particular, the work of its Faith and Order Commission, suggests that the biblical notion of *koinonia* provides a basis for bringing together

---

24. *Ibid*, Book 4, 1 10.
25. *Corpus Reformatum* 10 b, 309.
26. Calvin, *Institutes*, Book 4, 2 1.

basic ecclesiological perspectives which have emerged in ecumenical dialogues, which could lead to a shared vision of the nature, unity and mission of the church. Such shared emphases are the church as gift of the Word of God, the church as mystery or sacrament of God's love for the world, the church as the pilgrim people of God, the church as servant and prophetic sign of God's coming kingdom.[27]

This appears to presuppose the use of the idea of *koinonia* as a description of what might be termed an ecumenical consensus regarding the interdependence of divergent but self consistent ecclesiologies found in ecumenical discussions and dialogue groups.

In this context I offer my own reflections on this development in the light of what I have described as a Reformed ecclesiology, evinced in the writing of John Calvin.

Firstly, the word *koinonia* in the New Testament may be said to have two primary meanings. Primarily, it connotes participation in the mystery of the economy of salvation present in the world in the person of Jesus Christ. Secondarily, *koinonia* means fellowship with other Christians in that mystery of salvation present in the world in the person of Christ and the gift of the Holy Spirit. But it is fellowship on the ground of participation. The two senses are inseparable and interrelated. There is no fellowship except through participation in the mystery of Christ, but there is no participation without fellowship with other Christians. The primary meaning, to which I refer as participation in the mystery of Christ, may be seen in passages such as the following: Romans 6:8, 8:17, 6:6; 2 Timothy 2:12; 2 Corinthians 7:3; Colossians 2:12-13; Ephesians 2:5-6. Sharing in Christ comes about through the work of the Holy Spirit (2 Cor 13:13, Phil 2:1). The secondary meaning, fellowship with other Christians on the basis of fellowship or sharing in Christ, may be seen in such passages as 2 Corinthians

---

27. See 'Faith and Order Paper No 181', *The Nature and Purpose of the Church: A Stage on the Way to a Common Statement*, 1998.

8:23, Romans 15:27, 12:13, and Hebrews 10:33. The two senses are united in a trinitarian *koinonia* in which Christians participate, according to 1 John 1:3, 6, 3:2, 24, and 4:13.

The question arises in respect to what is indicated as the primary meaning of the word *koinonia* participation in the mystery of the economy of salvation present in the world in the person of Jesus Christ, whether this is at all a helpful way of describing comparative ecclesiologies. For it seems to me that it is precisely in terms of their understanding of *koinonia* in this primary sense that the ecclesiologies diverge significantly from each other. Let me illustrate what I think may be called this theological begging of the question. The use of such a methodology in ecumenical discussion runs the risk of finding complementarity rather than contradictions in divergent ecclesiologies.

In the *Dogmatic Constitution of the Church* of Vatican II the church is described as a sacrament. 'The church in Christ is in the nature of a sacrament—a sign and instrument, that is, of communion with God and of unity among all men' (Section 1). 'All those who in faith look towards Jesus, the author of salvation and the principle of unity and peace, God has gathered together and established as the church, that it may be for everyone the visible sacrament of this saving unity' (Section 9). 'Christ . . . sent his life giving Spirit upon his disciples and through him set up his Body which is the church as the universal sacrament of salvation' (Section 48).[28]

Now it is quite problematic from the point of view of Reformed theology to describe the church as sacrament. This is not because the Reformers, Luther as well as Calvin, undervalued the place of the sacraments in the life of the church. On the contrary, the Reformation confessions are highly critical of any such devaluation.

---

28. *Documents of Vatican II*, W M G Abbot ed, (London: Chapman, 1967).

We utterly condemn the vanity of those who affirm
sacraments to be nothing else than naked or bare
signs. No, we assuredly believe that by Baptism we
are engrafted into Christ Jesus, to be made partakers
of his righteousness . . . and also in the Supper rightly
used Christ Jesus is so joined with us that he becomes
the very nourishment and food of our souls . . . we are
so made flesh of his flesh and bone of his bones that,
as the eternal Godhead has given to the flesh of Christ
Jesus (which by its own condition and nature was
mortal and corruptible) life and immortality, so does
the flesh and blood of Christ Jesus eaten and drunk by
us give to us the same privileges (Scots Confession
1560, Ch XXI). [29]

At issue in the use of 'sacrament' as a description of the church,
in terms of Reformed ecclesiology, is not a devaluing of the
sacraments but the fact that such a description of the church
implies that faith which corresponds to God's gracious work of
salvation in Christ is changed into a human work. For when the
church is described in sacramental terms it is extending that
view of the church presupposed in the Council of Trent's
Canons on the most holy sacrifice of the Mass which define the
sacrament of the mass as the central mystery of the life of the
church. There the teaching of the Reformation is explicitly
anathematised in terms of those who 'teach that in the mass a
true and proper sacrifice is not offered to God . . . that the
sacrifice of the mass is merely an offering of praise and
thanksgiving . . . and is not propitiatory'. This is to be
understood in the sense that the bloody sacrifice of Jesus giving
up his life on the cross is re-presented by the unbloody action of

---

29. *Witness of faith: historic documents of the Uniting Church in Australia*,
    M Owen ed, (Melbourne: Uniting Church Press, 1984; contains:
    Basis of Union, The Apostles Creed, The Nicene Creed The Scots
    Confession of Faith, The Westminster Confession of Faith, The
    Savoy Declaration of Faith, John Wesley's sermons.

the priest. 'For it is one and the same victim: he who now makes the offering through the ministry of priests and he who then offered himself on the cross; the only difference is in the manner of the offering.'[30]

Here in the ministry of the priest the church is clearly understood in terms of an identity of action, albeit in a secondary sense. The primary acting subject, Jesus Christ, identifies himself with priestly action. For this reason, as Vatican II puts it in line with Pius XII, the ordained priesthood differs 'essentially and not only in degree from the common priesthood of all the faithful'.[31] Pius XII had called the priest *superiorum . . . populo* (superior to the people).[32] Accordingly, the liturgical action of the church is understood to be a *perficere* (perfecting) of the work of Christ. Certainly, it is Christ himself who accomplishes his work in the liturgy. But his work is an *opus perficiendum*, a work to be completed.[33]

This understanding of priestly action and, consequently, of the liturgical action of the church is one which sees the primary meaning of *koinonia* in a quite different sense than that which I have attempted to elucidate in terms of a Reformed ecclesiology. Here it would appear that the church's action in and through the priest, the church's liturgical action as such, has ascribed to it much more than simply testimony. For Calvin, as for Luther, the liturgical action of the church as such, or the priesthood as authorised by the church, is to be radically distinguished from God's action primarily because the meritorious work of Jesus Christ is definitively accomplished. It

30. See *Creeds of the Churches,* revised edition, J Leith ed, (Richmond, Virginia: John Knox Press, 1973), 399f.
31. *The Documents of Vatican II*, Dogmatic Constitution on the Church, Section 10.
32. *Mediator Dei* Encyclical of Pope Pius XII on the Sacred Liturgy, November 1947, Chapter 84.
33. *The Documents of Vatican II*, Constitution on the Sacred Liturgy, Section 10.

is not an *opus perficiendum* (a work to be completed) but, one might say, an *opus operatum* (a work performed). It has once for all won the forgiveness of sins.

The constitutive significance of God's Word for the Reformed understanding of the liturgical action of the church is a consequence of understanding the existence and life of the church to be dependent upon God's action alone. In this way it is impossible to confuse the action of the church with the action of God. The church does not complete but testifies to a completed event. In this sense the Reformed understood the church as the *ecclesia audens* (a hearing church). In this way they believed that the place of God as the primary acting subject in all that is said about the church and its relationship to God and the world is preserved. For Reformed ecclesiology, the church in all its speaking and acting does not cease to be *ecclesia audiens*, a church created by God's Word.

What would the recovery of a Reformed ecclesiology mean for the churches today? Primarily, it would entail rediscovering the basic insight into the distinction between God's work and the human work of witnessing to the truth of the divine economy of salvation fulfilled in Christ, and mediated by him as the ascended Lord through human witness in word and action. The church would be freed from its preoccupation with preserving its identity. The true identity of the church as the creation of the divine Word can be attested only by a community of witness which refuses to identify itself in any other way than as witness. Similarly, the structures of the church as a community of witness belong to an *ecclesia semper reformanda*. It is open to such reform as will help it more effectively to fulfil its fundamental task of witnessing to the gospel of Christ in specific historical, cultural and social circumstances.

Consequently, one must raise some question marks about the reception and use of *koinonia* as pointing a way forward in ecumenical dialogue. Seeing complementarity between various ecclesiologies may be of positive value in fostering fellowship, but it may also limit our awareness of significant differences between churches. A Reformed view of the church, while insisting on the distinction between the church as a creation of the Word and every empirical church, precisely as such sees no institutional form or church office as theologically necessary conditions for fellowship with other churches. It is open to an ecumenical practice which seeks to find shared rules for the exercise of the ministry of the Word as preaching and of the visible Word of the sacraments.

In seeking this fellowship we may be encouraged by the fact that in the seer's vision of the New Jerusalem there is not only no night, but also no temple; ecclesiology will be redundant!

'And I saw no temple in the city, for its temple is the Lord God the Almighty and the Lamb' (Rev 21:22).

The *Basis of Union* Considered as a Confessional Statement

In considering the matter of Christian unity it may well be true that

> ecclesiastical negotiations are but a fraction of the total work of Christian unity, for it includes all that happens in the renewal of the Churches in holiness, in worship, in theology, and in mission, and in the involvement of Christians with one another.[1]

But it is also true that ecclesiastical negotiations, the results of which are evinced by the *Basis of Union* for the Uniting Church in Australia, are to be considered as certainly not divorced from the life situation of the churches. Indeed, as will be shown, they are firmly riveted in the central activity of the church: its life of worship and prayer.

The thesis of this paper is that the development and form of the documents, related to the production of and including the *Basis of Union*, have a characteristic style which implies an ecclesiology that precludes the facile distinctions often drawn between theoretical and practical concerns in the matter of Christian unity.[2] We call this style confessional. This is to be clearly distinguished from confessionalism. This latter is concerned with factional interests. On the other hand, I am using confessional to mean that the *Basis of Union* presupposes

---

1. A M Ramsey, *Lambeth Essays On Unity* (London: SPCK, 1969), 4.
2. Particular note should be taken of the detailed discussion of the nature of confession in the church, which informed the thinking of the documents produced by the Joint Commission leading to the present *Basis of Union*. See *The Faith of the Church*, 1959, 22ff, 27ff; cf K Barth, *Church Dogmatics* 1/2 (Edinburgh: T&T Clark, 1956), 659ff, 591ff, and *The Church, Its Nature, Function and Ordering*, 1963, 12ff.

that disciplined thinking about church life and theology, as it relates to the question of Christian unity, cannot be done in some empty space. Theology is seen to have meaning within the definite context of particular historical circumstances where the Word of God comes to meet the church in the witness of Scripture and the church's tradition. This is the concrete ground where knowledge of God becomes actual within the *Una Sancta*. Thus speech about God according to this understanding of the confessional stance of the *Basis of Union* cannot be understood as a study in itself or *in abstracto*. The object (subject!) of this study is to be found only in the sphere of the actual faith and obedience of the church.

Whilst the confessional nature of the *Basis of Union* is not as obvious as that of the supporting documents—for purposes of brevity—yet it is true to say that in the critical paragraphs the *Basis* makes it quite clear from whence it derives its impetus and direction. In this connection it is to be noted that, in paragraph 3 dealing with the unity of the church and in paragraph 5 relating to the Scriptures, the *Basis* uses the word 'acknowledge'. By so doing, quite apart from what the actual paragraphs say, the authors wish to maintain that the subject matter of their confession arises out of a particular circumstance in the life of the church. It is our contention that much misunderstanding of the *Basis of Union* would be obviated if this fact were not consistently ignored by commentators. For not only is it the case that this word 'acknowledge' obviously infers that, although knowledge of God certainly does not come without our work, it does not come about through our work. What is even more important, with this word 'acknowledge' the *Basis of Union* confesses that in knowing God it does not comprehend how it comes to know what it confesses—it can only be ascribed to God whose self-giving compels this avowal.

It is not our intention to discuss further the theological epistemology of the *Basis of Union* considered as a confessional statement. Our purpose is to emphasise the importance, for assessing the *Basis of Union*, of taking into account the structure of such confessional material and the theological questions raised thereby.[3] For example, if it is true as stated in paragraph 3 of the *Basis of Union* that the unity of the church is 'acknowledged' to be built upon the unity of Jesus Christ, then it is important to realise that the two propositions—one concerning the unity of God's people, and the other concerning the unity of Jesus Christ the God-Man—presuppose an unexpressed factor deriving from the confessional nature of the statements. This factor is the assumption that the unity and coherence of such statements derives from and is addressed to the God before whom they are made and to whom they are offered. They derive their theological coherence from the fact that speech about the specific divine act presupposes that God is presently active as personal.[4] For this reason it is logically inept to draw conclusions from such statements which appear in the *Basis of Union*, which presuppose this context, without taking into account their highly peculiar character.

The confessional nature of the material presupposes that there is no middle term joining the propositions as they appear, since there is no univocal middle term embracing the unity of God and human being in Jesus Christ, and the unity of God and human beings, and human beings with each other, within the church. This logical discrepancy is to be emphasised at all costs if the confessional nature of the *Basis of Union* is to be appreciated. It is the same disjunction which St Basil says is to be 'observed in silence'—the apparent difficulty in understanding existing for 'readers' advantage'.[5] Here theological coherence can be expressed only if the unexpressed

3. On the following, see Metropolitan Emilianos of Calabria, 'Neglected Factors Influencing Unity', *Eastern Churches Review* 11/4, 1969: 386ff.

4. W Pannenberg, *Basic Questions in Theology*, vol 1 (London: SCM, 1970), 233.

5. Basil, 'De Spiritu Sancto', Section xxvii, *The Library of Nicene and Post-Nicene Fathers* (Grand Rapids: Eerdmans, 1894).

condition of the confessional statement is fulfilled, namely, that the theologian is the recipient of the free grace of Christ who in himself unites both God and human beings and human beings with each other. Here what Bonhoeffer maintains as basic to theological thought must be kept in view, that is, 'To speak of Christ, then, will be to speak within the context of the silence of the church'.[6]

What Rahner maintains as true of the church, as the fundamental sacrament, is here to be maintained as true of its theology. Since this 'silence', this logical discrepancy, this 'difficulty in understanding' which takes place for our benefit, exists to make plain that God's

> redemptive grace in Christ is free grace, his own operation in us and not a factual reality always of necessity present, and in regard to which it is really only a question for us, of what attitude we choose to adopt to it . . . This act of the church in regard to man necessarily bears within it the structure of the church's own nature.[7]

If the confessional structure of such statements as may be found in the *Basis of Union* are not appreciated in terms of the outline given above, then serious logical problems, which soon become theological problems will arise in any attempt at interpretation. For then the *Sitz im Leben* of the liturgy and therefore the peculiar logic of confessional statements will be ignored. It will then be assumed possible to survey the questions of the self-revealing God and human existence as two distinct entities, co-ordinating both according to a 'higher principle' whether realist or idealist, and attempting to define the differing roles of divine and human causality in redemption.

Referring briefly to paragraph 5 of the *Basis of Union*, it is to be observed that the authority of Scripture is understood within

---

6. D Bonhoeffer, *Christology* (London: Wm Collins, 1960), 27.
7. K Rahner, *The Church and the Sacraments* (London: Burns & Oates, 1963), 202.

a confessional framework. In contrast to the rationalism of similar statements which occur in the Westminster Confession, where authority is understood in terms of the scholastic distinction between created and uncreated grace, nature and supernature,[8] we see that in the *Basis of Union* authority is understood in personal rather than rationalistic terms. The prophets and apostles become authoritative because they are obedient recipients of God's self-giving in love and judgment. The Scriptures derive their authority when this relationship is repeated on the basis of their unique witness. In this way the *Basis* effectively excludes such authorities, whether in the form of the church's teaching office, pious self-consciousness or human reason, by which the church can recognise and evaluate revelation and form its own independent view.

According to the *Basis of Union* the church stands or falls with the fact that it obeys, is 'controlled' as the prophets and apostles were 'controlled'. Here it is a question of a relationship in which the church receives, in which it really has a Lord and belongs to him wholly and utterly. The nature of the authority here intended for the Scriptures is one where the unity and difference between God's Word and human words is heard in all of Scripture, and one that is very closely related in structure to the sacrifice of praise in liturgical ascriptions. Here too the unity of human words and their object (subject) is achieved in full consciousness of the fact that their meaning and truth is realised in God in ways completely beyond our comprehension.[9]

---

8. See *Creeds of Christendom*, P Schaff ed, (New York: Harpers, 1877), chs i & v, 600ff.
9. E Schlink, *The Coming Christ and the Coming Church* (Edinburgh: Oliver & Boyd, 1967), 41ff, 83, 85. Cf the instructive analysis of the same problem in the field of epistemology in M Polanyi, *Personal Knowledge* (Chicago: Chicago University Press, 1962), and *Knowing and Being* (London: Routledge, Keegan Paul, 1969). In relation to theological language, see G Ebeling, *Word and Faith,*

The Basis of Union Considered as a Confessional Statement

It is therefore obvious that unless the confessional nature of the material found in the *Basis of Union* is kept in view positive and critical discussion will be difficult. False questions will be raised and answers given which are quite irrelevant to the subject matter. It is certainly not suggested that there be no discussion of the contents. But unless serious note is taken of its basic structure much discussion will be beside the point. It may very well be that in learning the direction in which the *Basis of Union* invites us to look, we will have to oppose critically certain, or even many, of its statements!

(London: SCM Press, 1960), 407ff, and T F Torrance, *Theological Science* (London: Oxford University Press, 1969), 203ff, and T F Torrance *Christian Doctrine of God—One Being Three Persons* (Edinburgh: T&T Clark, 1996), 86ff.

Rebaptism? The Uniting Church in Australia and the Christian Tradition

In the New Testament both the act of proclaiming the gospel and the apostolic witness concerning the gospel are called 'tradition' or 'traditioning'. So when one speaks about tradition reference is not being made to some anachronistic, outmoded slavish attention to ancient ways of doing things, but to the way in which the church today 'traditions' the apostolic witness to the gospel of Jesus Christ.

The question before the Uniting Church in the issue of rebaptism is that of the Church's 'traditioning' of the gospel received from the apostles and the recognised teachers in the early church and from the Reformation. It is a question of the Uniting Church's unity and continuity with this tradition and therefore its 'catholicity'.

The Church always stands under the threat that it will lose its way and find another gospel than that which has been handed on to it by the Reformation in which the Uniting Church in Australia has the roots of its tradition. The verb used to describe Judas' act of betrayal (*paradidomi*, as in John 13:2 and parallels) comes from the same root as the noun meaning 'a handing over or down' (*paradosis*). This is the New Testament word for the tradition of the church regarding the apostolic witness to Christ as Lord.

As Luther rightly perceived in his work 'Against Rebaptism',[1] in this issue the Church faces the central issue of the gospel of God's free grace. As he maintains,

> All heretics do the same with the gospel. They perceive it wrongly and then hasten to make a new gospel.[2]

---

1. *Luther's Works*, vol 40 (St Louis: Concordia Publishing House, 1958), 229ff.

The central issue regarding 'rebaptism' is whether the Uniting Church, as heir of the Reformation, will identify its tradition as deriving from this source. Will it continue to hand down the gospel in unity and continuity with the Reformers? Paul commends the Corinthian Christians 'because you maintain the traditions even as I have handed them on to you' (1 Cor 11:2); what Paul himself 'had received from the Lord' he 'handed on' (traditioned) to them (11:23; 15:3). So we must constantly be alert to the nature of the 'traditioning' in all that the church says and does.

The Tradition Regarding Rebaptism for the Churches of the Reformation

An answer to this question will be illustrated from two perspectives, from the Lutheran and then from the Reformed or Calvinist tradition. In Luther's day those who promoted rebaptism were called '*ana*-baptists' which means simply those who insisted on 'baptism from above'. This was contrasted to the 'baptism from below' which was said by them to be practised by the church.

According to Luther the issue in the two views of baptism was that one view promoted reliance on good works in contrast to the other which celebrated the free grace or the gift of righteousness of Christ. Luther writes,

> There is a devil who promotes confidence in works among the Anabaptists. He feigns faith, whereas he really has a work in mind. He uses the name and the guise of faith to lead poor people to rely on a work. It is the devil's masterpiece when he can get someone to compel the Christian to leave the righteousness of Christ for a righteousness of works.
>
> So he tears people away from the righteousness of Christ, as if it were a vain thing, and leads them into rebaptising as if it were a better righteousness. He

---

2.   *Ibid*, 248.

> causes them to reject the former righteousness of
> Christ as ineffectual and to fall prey to a false
> righteousness. Whoever therefore permits himself to
> be rebaptised rejects the righteousness of Christ, of all
> things such behaviour is most horrible.[3]

The reason why the Anabaptists lead people astray, according
to Luther, is that they promote individual faith as something
that people can place their confidence in before God. Thus they
interpret a verse such as Mark 16:16, 'one who believes and is
baptised will be saved', to mean that no one should be baptised
but believers and that all other baptisms are false.

But according to Luther such a view places the Christian in
an impossible position regarding baptism. It means that no one
should be baptised unless they and the church are certain they
believe. Without that certainty the Anabaptist would be in the
same position as those whom they condemn—of baptising
without faith, for uncertain faith is the same as unbelief.

> I would compare the person who lets himself be
> rebaptised with the man who broods and has scruples,
> because he says to himself he did not believe when he
> was baptised as a child. So when the devil comes and
> tempts him about the certainty of his faith his heart is
> filled with scruples and he says, 'Now for the first time I
> feel I have the right faith; before I did not believe'. Then it
> happens again—'So I need to be baptised a third time, the
> second baptism being to no avail'. You think the devil
> can't do such things? You had better get to know him
> better. He can go on and cast doubt on the third or the
> fourth baptism and so on incessantly; just as he did to me
> on the matter of whether I had confessed all my sins. All
> this is nonsense.[4]

Luther maintains therefore that the most certain form of
baptism is child baptism. An adult may come to Christ as a
Judas and have himself baptised. But a child who comes to
Christ in baptism cannot deceive, just as John the Baptist came

---

3.   *Ibid*, 248.
4.   *Ibid*, 239.

in his mother's womb and received the word of the gospel through the mouth of Christ's mother.

To make baptism dependent upon the uncertainty and vagaries of our faith is to destroy the grace of Christ and the promise of the gospel that in Christ our human nature has been turned from darkness to light, from sin to righteousness. It is to deny that through baptism this righteousness is reckoned by God to be ours.

To the objection, 'Children cannot believe because they do not speak or have understanding', Luther replies, 'How can you be sure of this? What is the scripture by which you prove it?'[5]

There are, Luther says, Scripture passages which show that children do believe. For example, John was a child in his mother's womb when it says that he leapt for joy at Mary's greeting of his mother Elizabeth (Luke 1:41). If it is replied that John was an exception and that this is no proof that all baptised children have faith, this may well be so. But it is certain that the foundation of rebaptism is unsure in as much as it cannot be shown from Scripture that children cannot believe. Therefore the argument that children cannot believe is unscriptural.[6]

By various arguments Luther attempts to show the fallacious scriptural basis of the argument for rebaptism. More importantly, he demonstrates that those who advocate it turn the gospel into a righteousness of works and thus deny that which they attempt to affirm, that is, the Lordship of Christ in the church and the life of the Christian.

In the Reformed or Calvinist tradition of the Reformation we find a systematic argument for infant baptism and against rebaptism. First of all some examples from the documents mentioned in the *Basis of Union* of the Uniting Church in Australia, which are to be studied by the church's ministers and instructors so that their consciences may be informed.[7]

---

5.   *Ibid*, 241ff.
6.   *Ibid*.
7.   *The Basis of Union of the Uniting Church in Australia*, paragraph 10.

Westminster Confession 1647, Chapter 23

Baptism is a sign and seal of ingrafting into Christ, of regeneration, of remission of sins, and of being given up unto God, through Jesus Christ. Not only those who actually profess faith but also infants of one or both believing parents are to be baptised by the right use of this ordinance. The grace promised is not only offered, but really exhibited and conferred by the Holy Ghost . . . The sacrament of Baptism is but once to be administered to any person.

The Scots Confession 1560, Article 23

We damn the error of the Anabaptists, who deny baptism to be applied to children before they have faith and understanding. We assuredly believe that by baptism we are ingrafted into Jesus Christ, to be made partakers of his justice, by which our sins are covered and remitted.[8]

The Heidelberg Catechism 1563, Q 74

Are infants to be baptised? Yes. Since they as well as their parents belong to the covenant and people of God, and both redemption from sin and the Holy Spirit, who works faith, are through the blood of Christ promised to them no less than their parents. They are also by baptism, as a sign of the covenant, ingrafted into the Christian church.[9]

Uniting Church Assembly statement 1982

What is the relation between baptism and the personal response of the one baptised? The salvation promised and effected by baptism, depends upon the fact that once for all, the crucified, risen and ascended Christ has made effective the faithfulness of God to us and our response of faith to the Father. Our personal

---

8.   See *The Scots Confession* Article 21, in *Witness of Faith: Historic Documents of the Uniting Church in Australia*, M Owen ed, (Melbourne: Uniting Church Press, 1984), 73-74.

9.   For this and other Reformed catechisms see, T F Torrance, *The School of Faith* (London: J Clarke, 1959).

response does not add to Christ's faithfulness, but is
the means by which Christ's confession finds
expression within his Body.[10]

It is characteristic of the Reformed tradition of the Reformation
that baptism is understood within the context of God's gracious
covenant with Israel and, in Jesus Christ, with all people.[11]

Jesus Christ as the fulfiller of the covenant between God and
human beings is not simply a mighty act of God on behalf of
humanity, but an act of God which includes within it our
human response of faithfulness and love to God the Father. This
means that Jesus Christ is understood not simply as an agent or
instrument of salvation, but is himself its very substance.

What is promised in baptism is the saving reality of union
and communion with the Christ who throughout his earthly
life, from conception to death, perfected not only God's
faithfulness to sinful humanity, but the human response of faith
to God. He thus fulfils the covenant between God and
humanity in himself—from the point of view of God and from
the point of view of the human response to God. This he has
effected once and for all, sealing it with the blood of the cross
and being vindicated by the Father in his resurrection from the
dead.

The one who was raised from the dead promises himself to
us in the Holy Spirit. This is the same Spirit which he
received—not for his own sake but for ours—in his birth and
baptism and through which 'he offered himself without blemish
to God to purify our conscience from dead works to serve the
loving God' (Heb 9:14).

This view of baptism takes into account the significance of
the birth, life and death of Jesus. For in Jesus life there is
translated into this-worldly reality God's saving activity.

---

10. See *Minutes of the Third Assembly of the Uniting Church 1982*. Cf R
    Horsfield, *Baptism: An Evangelical Sacrament* (Melbourne: Uniting
    Church Press, 1984), 6ff.
11. See *Heidelberg Catechism* Q 74 and Calvin's *Geneva Catechism* Q 339,
    in T F Torrance, *op cit*.

Throughout his life he offered the perfect response to the Father in the Spirit of faith and obedience—again, not for his own sake but for ours. So in baptism the same Spirit which Christ received and in which he sanctified every stage of human development, unites us with this Christ. This happens in such a way that whatever stage of life we may be at, whether that of an infant or an adult, our human response to God is affirmed and upheld in spite of our weakness and frailty.

To practise rebaptism in this context would be to deny the saving significance of the humanity of Christ, of him as the one who fulfils the covenant with us and for us in relation to God. It would be to substitute, instead, our own faith or experience as the basis of our relationship to God, and thus to depend upon our work. It would be to turn God's gracious covenant into a contract and thus deny the sole sufficiency of Christ's incarnational obedience and atoning sacrifice, in which alone the covenant between God and human beings is sealed and made perfect.

It is appropriate to conclude this summary of the Reformed tradition and its teaching on baptism by emphasising its substance in the words of one who often had some strong things to say about the Calvinism he met in England in the eighteenth century, Charles Wesley:

> Jesus, let all my work be Thine,
> Thy work, O Lord, is all complete,
> And pleasing in the Father's sight;
> Thou only hast done all things right.[12]

It was in defence and celebration of this tradition that the Reformers rejected rebaptism.

---

12. *Methodist Hymn Book* No 572 (London Methodist Conference Office, 1933).

What is the Meaning of Holy Communion?

Why do we celebrate holy communion? The church does not exist of or by itself. The church lives because of Christ its Lord's relationship with it. The Uniting Church's *Basis of Union,* paragraph 4 states

> that the church is able to live and endure through the changes of history only because her Lord comes, addresses and deals with people in and through the news of his completed work . . . (He) brings into being what otherwise could not exist, (He) reaches out to command people's attention and awakens their faith . . . In His own strange way he constitutes, rules and renews them as his church.

The context, then, in which we are to seek an answer to the question 'What is the meaning of holy communion?' is found in the relationship between Christ and his church. A simple short answer may be given as to the reason why we celebrate holy communion. We celebrate holy communion because our Saviour, Jesus Christ, *commanded* us to do so. 'Do this in remembrance of me' (Luke 22:19). This is his own appointed way of meeting with and constituting his people as his church, on its way to meet him in history at his final appearing. Then we shall no longer need a sacrament,[1] though we shall still worship.

However we may give two further reasons why the relationship between Christ and his church takes the form indicated by the Lord's supper.

In Christ his word and his action are one. His action and his speaking are coincidental with his being who he is as the Son of

---

1.   Cf the vision of Revelation 21:22: 'And I saw no temple in the city, for its temple is the Lord God the Almighty and the Lamb'.

God. But in his relationship to us, these are held partially apart in order to make room for our personal response of faith. We may illustrate this by looking at the incident in which Jesus healed the paralysed man who was let down through the roof by his friends when they could not get near to Jesus. Jesus kept apart his word *of forgiveness* and his action of healing in order 'that you may know that the Son of man has authority on earth to forgive sins' (Matt 9:6). He makes room for knowledge and faith in relationship with himself. He does not treat us as objects. Jesus also speaks in a number of parables of a householder or a king going into a far country, there spending time and then returning to reckon up with his servants (see Luke 19:12; Matt 25:14). These parables have reference not only to God's relationship with Israel in the light of Jesus coming, but apply also to the time of the church between Christ's ascension and his final coming. Jesus' institution of the Lord's Supper or holy communion clearly shows that he envisaged a long period of time, a period of waiting in which the church would grow and develop in union and communion with himself. Thus the relationship he institutes between himself and his people provides for his presence with them in such a way that takes account that it is not yet consummated in its fullness. The Holy Communion 'provides the church with travelling provisions on the way to the final inheritance of the Kingdom'.[2]

Therefore the reason why we celebrate holy communion is to be sought, firstly, in the way in which Christ wills to be with and for his people on the way to the final revelation of his glory.

Secondly, the reason why we celebrate holy communion in the particular form in which Christ has given it to us is to be sought in the *condescension of Christ to our weakness.* In his relationship with us he takes account of our frailty and

---

2. *The Church: Its Nature Function and Ordering.* Second report of the Joint Commission on Church Union (Melbourne: Aldersgate Press, 1963), 24ff.

accommodates himself to it. John Calvin emphasised this aspect in his 'Short Treatise on the Lord's Supper'.

> For seeing we are so foolish, that we cannot receive him with true confidence of heart, when he is presented by simple teaching and preaching he has attached to his Word a visible sign, by which he represents the substance of his promises, to confirm and fortify us, and to deliver us from all uncertainty.[3]

The form of the holy communion thus speaks to us of the inestimable mercy of God who in Christ takes account of our bodily weaknesses so that we may appropriate the truth of his life; by which the church is sustained through all the vagaries of historical change.

Who is Communicated in Holy Communion?

In seeking to answer this question it is important that we ask it in this form. We ask not what, but who is communicated. The answer to the question 'what' will give rise to answers which have been the seeds of division within the church since earliest times. The 'what' question assumes an answer which can be understood in relation to other known objects or subjects. The 'who' question assumes that an answer can be given only in terms of a confession of faith in which our human words are opened up by him to whom they refer, so that the mystery of Christ's gracious presence with his people remains.[4]

The Basis of Union (paragraph 8) states that in the holy communion the people of God 'have communion with their Saviour' (see 1 Cor 10:16-17). Here it is assumed that in the communion Christ himself is present as both the giver and the gift of the sacrament. We may understand this more clearly if

---

3.   J Calvin, *Treatise on the Lord's Supper* (Philadelphia: Westminster Press, 1954), 144.

4.   See D Bonhoeffer, *Christology* (London: Collins, 1966), 28ff, and J Torrance *Worship, Community and the Triune God of Grace* (Carlisle: Paternoster Press, 1996).

we look at one aspect of the biblical account of the institution of the Lord's supper (see Mark 14:24 and parallels). Jesus speaks here of the cup as the 'covenant', or in the alternative reading, 'new covenant in his blood'.

An adequate appreciation of the intention of Jesus here must take account of the essential pattern of the covenant in the Old Testament. There the covenant was seen to be based upon the promise of God to be Israel's Lord. 'I will be your God and you shall be my people' (Lev 26:12; Jer 11:4; 30:22). It was in the fulfilment of this covenant, in terms both of God's faithfulness to Israel and Israel's faithful response to God, that the prophets sought the destiny of God's people (Jer 31; Isa 53).

Jesus speaks of *his* blood as the mode of redemption in direct relationship to the covenant between God and God's people, the covenant which remains broken from Israel's side. He offers his life in an act of sacrifice by which God's people may *share* in the covenant relation now fulfilled not only from the side of God and God's faithfulness but from the side of Israel's response as well. For Jesus is not only the Word of God to Israel; he is also the word of Israel's faithful and loving response to God. It is this fulfilled covenant with Israel, consummated in Jesus' life, death and resurrection, that the early church saw as now made available to Gentiles as well.

Jesus' gift of the blood of the covenant in his sacrificial death, which was impending at the last supper, reposes on the fact that throughout his whole earthly life, but above all in his death, there was worked out in the union of God and Israel's flesh in his person, the fulfilment of the covenant relationship. From birth to death Jesus took our broken, sinful humanity, and through his life of prayer and supplication 'with tears' (Heb 5:7) he bent our unruly wills back into union and communion with his Father. The covenant between God and Israel was thus made anew when, in the fulfilment of his obedience for our sake, he accepted the bitter cup of divine judgment in such a marvellous manner that the judge became the judged, in perfect obedience to the Father's will.

The typical passages which speak of Christ's faithfulness in this way (Rom 3:21-25; Gal 2:16; 2:20; 3:22) show us the difference between the Old and the New Covenant. Like the Old Testament, the New Testament emphasises the faithfulness of God which requires from human beings a corresponding faithfulness. In the gospel, the 'good news' is that the faithfulness of God has achieved its end or purpose in the faithful response of Jesus to his Father's loving purpose for all people. He is the embodiment of all peoples' faithful response in covenant with God. Philippians 3:9 speaks of Christians not having a righteousness of their own based on law, but based on or 'through the faith of Christ'.[5] This is summed up in 2 Corinthians 1:18ff according to which Jesus Christ is not only the faithful 'Yes' of God to humanity; he is also the faithful 'Amen' of our human response to God.

By this action of Jesus at the last supper we are to understand that, in terms of the covenant relationship between God and Israel and the Church, there takes place what John Calvin called a *mirifica commutatio* or 'wonderful exchange'. This exchange has been made by

> his boundless goodness. Having become with us the Son of man, he has made us with himself sons of God. By his own descent to the earth he has prepared our ascent to heaven. Having received our mortality, he has bestowed upon us his immortality. Having undertaken our weakness, he has made us strong in his strength. Having submitted to our poverty, he has transferred to us his riches. Having taken upon himself the burden of unrighteousness with which we were oppressed, he has clothed us with his righteousness.[6]

---

5. My translation of the genitive *pisteos Christou*. Compare K Barth, *The Epistle to the Philippians* (London: SCM, 1962), 99ff.

6. *Institutes of the Christian Religion*, Book 4, Ch 17, Sec 2 (reprinted, Grand Rapids: Eerdmans, 1975, vol 2).

Thus the promise which Jesus attaches to the bread and the wine of holy communion is that he here offers h*imself* to us in such a way that in our receiving of him we are constituted God's people covenanted in him. We become the church, which is the very Body of Christ.

What Benefits are Communicated?

It is only after we have sought an answer to the question 'Who is communicated in holy communion?' that we can properly ask the question as to its benefits. For it is not *we* who define our need before God, in terms of our religious feelings or lack of them, but we must understand who we are and therefore our need in terms of God's action in Christ in relationship to us. Therefore our answer to the question what benefits are communicated to us in the holy communion can only be another form of answering the question as to who is communicated to us. For the benefits or gifts of holy communion are identical with the giver, who is Christ himself.

Thus our Reformation ancestors condemned those who, because of their understanding of their religious capacities, did not believe it was necessary to speak of the bread and wine of the holy communion as anything more than symbols of *our* faith relationship to Jesus, a relationship which existed apart from them.

> We utterly condemn the vanity of those who affirm
> the sacraments to be nothing else than naked or bare
> signs.[7]

We can become so interested in the benefits of holy communion that we separate them from the reality of Christ's promised presence with us by the means which he has chosen. We must see the benefits of holy communion to consist primarily in our

---

7. *The Scottish Confession of Faith*, ch 21; *Reformed Confessions of the 16th Century*, A Cochrane ed, (London: SCM, 1966).

receiving the life of Christ and his righteousness through the gift of the Holy Spirit.

It is the Holy Spirit who unites us to Christ in the holy communion. He is given to us by Christ as the Spirit in which he gained the victory over sin and death for our sakes. We come to communion with empty hands and mouths and the Holy Spirit assimilates us into the all-sufficient work of Christ, and the Father looks on us only as we are found in him; so that we receive and are filled with all the goodness of God.

It must not be thought that the Spirit acts in the place of, as in the absence of Christ; in the Spirit's coming Christ himself acts for us not only from the side of God toward us human beings, but also from our human side toward God. It is in the Spirit that we have these benefits, but the church is not the Body of the Spirit but the Body of Christ. There was no incarnation of the Spirit. It is precisely because of Christ's reception of the Spirit in our humanity for our sake, from his birth and baptism to his offering of himself on the cross,[8] that in him we were given the Spirit that is poured out on the church by the risen and glorified Lord. So by the Spirit the church

> does so eat the body and drink the blood of the Lord Jesus that He remains in them and they in him; they are so made flesh of his flesh and bone of his bone that as the eternal Godhead has given to the flesh of Christ Jesus, which by nature was corruptible and mortal, life and immortality, so the eating and the drinking of the flesh and blood of Christ Jesus does the like for us.[9]

---

8. Hebrews 9:14: 'How much more shall the blood of Christ, who through the eternal Spirit offered himself without blemish to God, purify your conscience . . .'

9. *Scottish Confession of Faith*, ch 21.

How Do We Understand Our Worship in the Service of Holy Communion?

The writer of the Epistle to the Hebrews describes Christ our Lord as the *leitourgos*—(8:23)—the 'leader of our worship'. The *leitourgia* or worship of Jesus is contrasted with the *leitourgia* of humans. Worship of him as our great High Priest is that which God has provided for human beings, and which alone is acceptable to God. Therefore all our worship is offered 'in the name of', 'through', 'in', 'for the sake of' Jesus Christ. *The question we have to ask of our services of holy communion is whether they help or hinder people's apprehension of the ministry and worship of Jesus Christ.*

This question was at the heart of one of the important disputes at the time of the Reformation. It was formulated in relation to holy communion or the mass: was it to be considered a sacrifice or not? On the one side the Roman Catholic church taught that in holy communion the action of the priest was an offering, in the bread and wine, a repetition of the sacrifice of Christ on the cross. This happened in such a way as to make the merit of Christ before the Father efficacious for those who received the elements. Thus the Council of Trent, in its reformulation of the Roman Catholic doctrine, stated that in the Mass

> the same Christ is contained and immolated who on the altar of the cross once offered himself in a bloody manner. The holy synod teaches that this is truly propitiatory. For it is one and the same Victim, the same one now offered by the ministry of priests as He who then offered Himself on the Cross, the manner of offering alone being different.[10]

---

10. Session 22, Canon 2. See F Hildebrand, *I Offered Christ* (London: Epworth Press, 1967), 5.

Against such a view the Reformers taught that the holy communion is not a *work* which the priest representing the church performs, but is wholly a gift which the church receives.

> Men, out of their own head, invented that it (the mass) is a sacrifice by which we obtain the remission of our sins before God. This is a blasphemy which is intolerable. If we do not confess Jesus Christ to be the sole sacrificer, or as we commonly call it Priest, by whose intercession we are restored to the Father's favour, we despoil him of his honour and do him grave hurt.[11]

Here we must draw a clear distinction in our understanding of the service of Holy Communion between 'propitiatory sacrifice' and 'eucharistic sacrifice'. Christ alone has offered to God the Father, once for all (Rom 6:10; also Heb 10:12), a propitiatory sacrifice in his obedient life and death. As we are united to him in our baptism and the eucharist we participate in Christ as members of his body, the church. In him we are offered to God, and Christ as the one great high priest intercedes in our name with the Father and brings us his word of peace and forgiveness. We may say, then, that in the eucharist we are offered to God and each other in the bread and wine as we are united to Christ. This offering up of ourselves in the bread and wine is not a work which we undertake, but a gift which we receive. For Christ's once for all propitiatory sacrifice cannot be repeated by us or the church (see Heb 7:27 and parallels).

This dispute about the nature of our worship still has unconscious echoes in our churches today. Some congregations sit to receive the holy communion whilst others may kneel. The former posture was adopted to protest the practice whereby Christ's benefits were made present by the action of the priest at the altar; the people knelt to adore the miracle. It also emphasised that at holy communion the family of God is gathered at the table of the Lord to receive from him the

---

11.   J Calvin, *Treatise on the Lord's Supper, op cit*, 155.

nourishment that joins them to each other and their Lord. On the other hand the practice of kneeling does not necessarily involve the adoration of the mass whereby the church adores its own action in the person of the priest, and is thus guilty of idolatry. Kneeling appropriately recognises the extraordinary mystery and wonder of Christ's gracious presence with us in the holy communion, and the fact that at the Lord's table we are always beggars. As Charles Wesley reminds us,

> No good word, or work, or thought
> Bring I to gain thy grace;
> Pardon I accept unbought,
> Thine offer I embrace;
> Coming, as at first I came,
> To take, and not bestow on Thee:
> Friend of sinners, spotless lamb,
> Thy blood was shed for me.[12]

The holy communion is a thanksgiving in which, together with our prayer and praise, we offer ourselves to God in the name of Jesus Christ by whom we are united to each other in his Body and called into the service of the world. It is also a *memorial*. At the last supper Jesus said, 'This do in remembrance of me' (Luke 22:19). The word remembrance (*anamnesis*) has rich liturgical significance in the Bible.[13] When Jesus commands the disciples to remember, he does not simply mean an act of recalling some remote event. At the holy communion we do not remember the passion of Christ as an isolated event long ago. Rather, we remember that we are the people whose sins Jesus confessed on the cross. Thus, for example, after the commandments in holy communion (Service No 1), we confess our sins 'through Jesus Christ our Lord'.

We remember that Christ our High Priest not only fulfilled the law for our sakes. He confessed our sins from the beginning

---

12. See Hildebrand, *op cit*, 37.
13. See the article 'Remembrance' by J K S Reid, *Church Service Society Annual*, May 1960.

of his life to the cross. Matthew 3:15 speaks of his submission to a baptism of repentance *for the forgiveness of sins*. The holy Son of God maintains that this is 'fitting', for in this way 'all righteousness is to be fulfilled', not for his own sake but for ours. He therefore does what is 'right' by placing himself in the wrong before God! We remember that we are the people for whom God has made a new covenant in the blood of Christ; *we* are the people whose sorrows Jesus bears as he intercedes for us and constitutes himself as the eternal memorial for us before God. 'Jesus, remember me' (Luke 23:42).

This work of realising, through remembrance, our participation in Christ's ministry for us all, as the one who constitutes himself as our covenantal relationship with God, is not so much a matter of us reminding ourselves of these events, but of Jesus Christ bringing his passion to our remembrance through the Holy Spirit. As Charles Wesley prayed at communion,

> Come, Thou witness of his dying;
> Come Remembrancer divine. (AHB, 429)

Clearly, we do not remember an absent Christ; in the Spirit he is present to bring the things we celebrate to our remembrance in an act of communion. So in all the parts of the communion service, the prayers, the reading and hearing of God's Word, our response of faith and self-offering in praise and thanksgiving, the church seeks to set forth the truth for us of our great High Priest. For it is in him that our humanity is presented to and united with the Father.

> He pleads His passion on the tree
> He shows Himself to God for me
> His prevalence with God declare. (C Wesley,
> Methodist Hymn Book, 232)

He lifts up our hearts and minds to God and opens the kingdom of heaven to all believers. Thus our worship does not bear witness to ourselves, as a form of psychological self-expression, but to Christ and what the world is in him and shall become through him. For the Christ who is present with us in the union of Holy Communion is the one who promises that in his final revelation we shall see that the kingdoms of this world are the kingdoms of our God and of his Christ. Therefore we proclaim the Lord's death in the Holy Communion 'till he comes' (1 Cor 11:26). For though we do not yet see all things subject to God, 'we see Jesus' (Heb 2: 9). As he presses forward to his final appearing, the church's worship naturally finds expression in its mission. The church invites all creatures to participate in our Lord's glorifying of the Father and thus to realise their created destiny in the Spirit.

Even so, 'Come, Lord Jesus' (Rev 22:20).

Part Three

Christian Ethics for God's World

The Church's Responsibility for the World: a Reformed Perspective

The context and the question of the following contribution was the theological sub-committee of the Hospital Task Group (Uniting Church of Australia, Queensland) attempt to bring to bear the church's understanding of its faith upon the issue of the church's involvement in health care through the specific form of owning hospitals. In order to appreciate the complexity of the issues involved it is important that the *context* in which the question is being discussed is agreed and, secondly, that the *question* that is being examined is understood.

The *context* in which the issue of the church's relationship to health care, in particular hospitals, is raised mitigates against the church's actions being understood. The contemporary context in which the church is set is conditioned by the eighteenth century movement in European thought known as the Enlightenment and by its consequences for our present self-understanding.

The major consequence has been to the creation of a mental world with which we become familiar before we can articulate its meaning. It is a world in which the 'knowing subject' defines external reality in terms of 'objective facts'. These 'objective facts' are 'value free', since they are the same for every reasonable person. These 'facts' are understood to be the determinate of truth. With unprecedented zeal the Enlightenment proposed to explain the world as something that is without purpose. The idea of purpose, as of any other 'value', is understood to belong to the 'subjective' sphere and is to be excluded as a determinate of truth precisely on the ground that it is a subjective variable. This dichotomy between fact and value, the explanation of everything in terms of antecedent causes according to a mechanistic model of reality, and the relegation of values to the privatised sphere of the individual subject is the Enlightenment's most characteristic and influential legacy. Enlightenment thinkers zealously pursued the idea of the methodological elimination of purpose from the study of the human, to the extent that it is assumed in our culture to be a universally valid maxim.

The public world, the world of economic relationships, is the world of facts; these are the same for everybody irrespective of their private values. The private world of values is that sphere where all are free to choose their own meaning which may interpret the facts. The question then arises whether Christian truth claims about human persons and their place in the world is simply another voice in a universal debating chamber, a night in which all cats are grey. Or is there a way of expressing Christian truth claims as public truth, that is to say, claims which refer to the public world of facts, for example, the nature of the human person. These claims have a particular form and a structure since their intelligibility is derived from, and grounded in, the nature of a world made to be in relationship with a personal God.

The Church's Relationship to the World

We cannot understand the relationship between the church and the world as one between two different realities, the 'sacred' and the 'secular'. There are not two realities but one which is defined by the action of God in God's self revelation in Jesus Christ. He it is who defines the nature of the church and the world in their relationship and difference, since he is both the creator Word and the incarnate Word who reconciles the world to God, so fulfilling the divine purpose for creation.

We begin to see what this means when we turn to explaining the significance of the relationship between creation and covenant in the Bible. Israel believed that God's actions in relationship to it as a people ran parallel to God's actions in relationship to the world. God leads the world, like Israel, out of the threatening watery chaos and brings forth the dry land as a cosmos. God gives the land to humans as their habitation, just as God gave the land of Canaan to God's people as their home. Stamped by their saving experience of God through their exodus from Egypt and the gift of the land, the Israelites' understanding of the world as God's creation entailed that they saw the world not as a self enclosed series of random events featuring an eternal cycle of ultimate meaninglessness. On the contrary, just as their history was understood to be guided by God's redemptive purpose, so also the world had a history, a purpose. Consequently, Israel historicised the creation myths borrowed from their cultural and ethnic neighbours; they turned them into accounts which related not abstract and timeless ideas but the history of the world and Israel's place as God's people in that world.

God's presence and activity in the world, as in relationship to Israel, preserves its being and safeguards it against a return to the chaos of disorder over which God triumphed in the beginning. God preserves Israel and safeguards it as God's people from the threat of annihilation by natural catastrophes such as the desiccating wilderness and the flood. Similarly, God negates the powers which reach into the life of the world as reminders of the fragility of its existence. It is dependent every moment that it exists on God's gracious care.

But the faith of Israel as expressed in the writings of the Old Testament do not merely testify to the Exodus experience and the consequent faith in God as the Creator of the world. They also witness to the hope of a future in which creation will be renewed by God's action which will reveal the final triumph over all that inimical to God's purposes and therefore negates the life of God's creature.

While this vision of a renewed creation echoes the experience of the initial exodus from Egypt it goes beyond simply recalling that fact. Isaiah 48:12 says those that go out will neither hunger nor thirst; their path is easy because all barriers have been cleared away. In Isaiah 49:11 nature itself will participate in this future liberation of God's people. The

133

mountains will break forth into rejoicing and the trees will clap their hands (Isa 49:13; 55:12). Waters will spring forth in the wilderness and streams in the desert (35:6). All nations will see this and know that the God of Israel is the God of their salvation (41:11: 42:17; 45:14ff). This eschatological vision fulfils the original creation. The exodus out of the chaos of slavery and the present world existing under the threat of chaos, preserved from the waters above the firmament and the encroaching threat of the sea by God's providential care, will be followed by the transfiguration of creation in the unveiled presence of God.

It was through Israel's understanding of itself as called and chosen by God through its particular historical experience that it came to recognise its gracious God as the Creator of the world. The classic expression of God's covenanted relationship with Israel is found in Exodus 20:1-2.

This aspect of Israel's experience of God has important implication for our understanding of the nature of created reality. The world created by God in freedom is not simply a contingent entity but is made to be the sphere in which God can establish a personal relationship with the creature. Thus the being of the world is one in which the personal relationship willed by God with the creature has priority over the impersonal.[1]

To know the God of Israel is to know that one's own existence and that of the world are created for relationship with others, with God and other human beings. This is the fundamental grammar of creation and it is seen already in the covenant established between God and Israel. The law, given to Israel as a sign of the covenanted relationship, has its basic character configured in terms of God's claim upon Israel in their relationship with God and the neighbour. What has been called the two tables of the law indicate that God's purposes for Israel focus on their relationship with God and their relationship with

---

1. See J Zizioulas, 'Human capacity and Incapacity', *Scottish Journal of Theology* 28, 1975: 401-444.

each other. The important Hebrew word *shalom* (peace) is a word used in the context of the covenant relationship of God with Israel. *Shalom* is realised in a community. The people of Israel were primarily a community not a state. When the state, the monarchy and the priesthood became 'powers', this was detrimental to Israel as God's covenanted community. These led to divisions, discrimination, oppression and poverty; to the absence of *shalom*.

The creation narratives depict human beings as essentially related to God, to each other and the earth. These relationships are in turn interrelated. What happens in the relationship of people with God affects their relationship with each other and the earth. The primary relatedness of which the Bible speaks is that by which humans are referred to God. This relationship is constitutive of what being human means. They are related to God by the sheer fact of their existence. God does not first create humans and then relate to them. The decision to create human beings in relationship to God is made by God prior to their creation (Gen 1:26). Genesis 5 and 10 indicate in their recitation of the *toledoth* of human generations after Adam and after Noah that the relatedness of human beings to God extends to all generations, to all people, and to all times. Human beings remain related to God even and precisely when they are shown to be hostile to God.

God's will is revealed to humans in the form of command, which means that the relationship they have with God is not a fate which overtakes them by the mere fact that they exist. It implies that the relationship between God and the creature is established by God in freedom and thus entails an act of will. Humans may or may not remain in communion with God. So God calls them to account. In Genesis 3 God asks, 'Who told you you were naked?', 'Where are you?', 'What have you done?' The human creature has the right of reply, as distinct from animals, such as the serpent.

Human beings are not only accountable to God for their relationship to God, but also for their actions in relation to each other. Genesis 9 implies that anyone who murders another human being has to answer to God for the blood that is shed.

The accountability we find in the biblical story is not the law of retribution as found in the Greek tragedians' account of relationships between gods and human beings. There the transgressors are punished by an inevitable fate. In the biblical account the relationship between God and human beings is one which involves a freedom that is characteristic of interpersonal relationships. God decides personally on the consequences of human sin; God's mind can change, God can repent; God can choose to be answerable for human beings' wrong doing. God chooses to be answerable for the blood of the fratricide Cain.

The Bible sees human dignity and worth grounded in a relationship established by God with human beings prior to and independent of any human action in the act of creation. Although this relationship is corrupted by human sin it is upheld and confirmed by God's action in both judgment and grace.

Jesus Christ and His Messianic Community

The transition from the people of God under the old covenant to the people of God under the new covenant came through the action of God in the birth, life, death and resurrection of Israel's Messiah, Jesus the Christ, thus fulfilling Israel's history.

The Christian church can never overlook the fact which St John states plainly. 'You worship what you do not know; we worship what we know, for salvation is from the Jews' (John 4:22). This is also the intent of St Paul's argument in Romans 11:17ff.

In the first act of his public ministry Jesus submits himself to the baptism of repentance proclaimed by John the Baptist. This was a baptism of repentance for the remission of sins. He who is the holy Son of God voluntarily identifies himself with the sin of Israel God's covenanted people. At this moment Jesus' action is publicly confirmed by the Father in the sending of the Holy

Spirit to rest upon Jesus. He who is ever one with the Father and the Spirit , who is God by nature and does not need to be given the Spirit, nevertheless submits himself, in identification with the flesh of fallen Israel, to this dependency upon the gift and promise of God (cf Phil 2:7-11). Jesus thus receives the Spirit not for his own sake but for the sake of all those whom he represents in the flesh he assumed from Mary—all Israel.

In receiving the Spirit vicariously, within the fallen flesh of Israel he had assumed from Mary, Jesus assumes responsibility before God for what God finds Israel to be in relation to God's self. He assumes responsibility for Israel as the breaker of God's covenant! He thus bears within himself the contradiction between God's holiness and the rebellion of human beings against God, this in the form of the flesh of Israel. Jesus' Baptism was thus his consecration to the whole course of his life and ministry as the incarnate Son of God. It prefigures in dramatic fashion the intimate connection between Jesus' life and death. His death was not the unhappy ending of an otherwise happy religious life. Jesus' death was the fulfilment of the purpose of his obedience as the Son of God. His obedience was to be this one thing; God in the *flesh*, with all that that involved in terms of his being rejected both by God and his fellow human beings.

It is this connection between Jesus' incarnation and his cross, between the incarnation and the atonement, that provides the basis for understanding the continuity and discontinuity between the Old and the New Covenants.

Under the Old Covenant God provides, in a unilateral fashion, the means of Israel's response in the context of its alienation and estrangement from God. Thus through the cult and the law God promises to be Israel's saviour and Lord. The blood of the sacrifice on the Day of Atonement[2] is God's gift and offering provided for the people. The prohibition on the eating of blood is precisely because the blood of all created

---

2.   Leviticus chaps 23ff.

things is equivalent to their life, which is God's as the Creator and author of all life. Enshrined in the law is God's promise, 'I will be your God and you shall be my people'.[3] In the gift of the law God promises God's self to Israel, takes responsibility for them as the recipients of the law, and therefore as the breakers of the law. In the cult and the law we thus see the provisional form of God's purpose in establishing the covenant with God's people. They were the God-provided means of a continuing relationship with a sinful people, and through this people with the world of humanity. The cult and the law were the God provided means of God remaining just in and for God's self and also remaining faithful to a faithless people at one and the same time.

In Jesus Christ the long relationship between God and Israel under the covenant comes to an end, in the sense of it being fulfilled. In him the Word and will of God is actualised in human existence.

Jesus himself is the form of the New Covenant since he *is* the New Covenant. He is the God who draws near to sinful humanity in judgment and forgiveness, bearing in himself the cost of human redemption. At the same time he is also the Human Being who responds to God's faithfulness with fidelity and trust, love and obedience: God's will is translated into human flesh, as the cult and the law testified under the Old Covenant. The Covenant and its institutions, the cult and the law, are now no longer aspects of an external relationship between God and human beings, but are identical with the being and life of the Son of God.

We are therefore to think that in Jesus' whole life, death and resurrection, as he passes through every stage of human development, there takes place in him a reconstitution or recreation of humanity in relationship to God. God in Christ recreates the relationship between God's self and the creature in such a manner that it is not something that takes place, as it

---

3.   Cf Exodus 6:7; Jeremiah 7:23.

were, above our heads in some external way. Rather, God penetrates to the depths of our human condition and bears in God's own self the cost of our redemption. He is, as John the Baptist proclaimed in John 1:29, 'the Lamb of God who takes away the sin of the world!'

This does not happen by means of some forensic conjuring trick. Jesus, as God's own Son, bears in himself the godforsakenness of the human condition. From the first act of his public ministry there is marked out the way of the cross and the resurrection. Through his obedient penitence on behalf of sinners and through his healing of the diseased humanity which clung to him at every turn, he presses forward to the goal of his life and embraces the cross as its fulfilment (cf Heb 2:10-17; 5:7-9). Thus in Jesus the Covenant is fulfilled, both from the side of the God who gives and promises God's self to the creature, and from the human side since there is found in him an obedient human 'Amen' to the judgment and the love of God.

If this is the case, we must consider the New Covenant to be not something external to who Jesus Christ is for our sake; it is identical with who he wills to be for us. This means that the church cannot be a holy society dedicated to perpetuating the memory of a great religious teacher. Rather, it exists as a community 'in Christ' (cf 2 Cor 5:17; Gal 3:26; 5:6; Eph 2:10; Col 1:4; 1:24; 1Thess 4:16; Heb 3:14). The church's life inheres in the person of Jesus Christ, the Son of God.

The Relationship Between the Church and God's Promised Future for Creation

The claim is made by the gospel of St John that the incarnate Son of God is the universal Word of God who was in the beginning with God and without whom nothing that was created came to be. This Word of God is the foundation of the created intelligibility of the world. The *logos* is the light which enlightens every person who is born into the world. This *logos* became flesh; 'flesh' in the Genesis narrative is a relational term binding humankind together as one kin as well as linking humankind with all living creatures.

At the same time the word 'flesh' establishes the basic distinction between God and human creatures. By the incarnation the condescension of God identifies God's own self with 'flesh'. In the gospel of St John 'flesh' does not mean humanity in any abstract neutral sense, but humanity in organised opposition to God. The faithfulness of God is such that God takes personal responsibility for the human creature in its turning away from God by assuming its flesh in the person of God's Son.

The incarnation of the Son of God indicates the manner in which God wills to reconstitute the relationship between God's self and the creature, and between human beings and other creatures. In contrast to Adam, Christ did not strive to be 'like God', though he was by nature God. He 'emptied himself' (Phil 2:7). He let go of his natural God-likeness in order to make himself one with Adam's flesh. The upward striving of Adam is reversed by the condescension of God. And in this self-humiliation of God consists the exaltation of the human creature.

In contrast to the first Adam, Christ 'trusts every word that proceeds from the mouth of God', rather than listen to the suggestion of the tempter (Matt 4:11). In contrast to the first Adam, Christ did not seek to justify himself over against God and other human beings; he remains silent before Pilate (Matt 26:63; Mark 14:61; cf Acts 8:32). In this way he bears eloquent testimony to the fact that he takes responsibility for the condition of the flesh with which, by his incarnation, he identifies himself. Consequently, he is accurately described by John the Baptist as 'the lamb of God who takes away the sin of the world' (John 1:29).

He makes himself one with sinners by submitting, at the hand of John the Baptist, to a 'baptism of repentance for the forgiveness of sins'. He 'fulfils all righteousness' by placing himself in the wrong before God (Matt 3:13-14). St Paul even says that Jesus Christ becomes a 'curse' (Gal 3:13).

Unlike Cain he sheds no innocent blood but allows his innocent blood to be shed. His blood, unlike that of Abel, does not cry out for vengeance but for mercy (Heb 12:24). Unlike Cain's descendent Lamech, who would avenge seventy times for an injury (Gen 4:16-24), he prays for forgiveness for those who take his life; he instructs his disciples to forgive seventy times seven.

The narrative of Genesis 1-11 helps us to appreciate the New Testament conviction that in the person of Jesus Christ there is present in the world *God's work of recreation whereby all the dismal consequences of the archetypal human temptation to be 'like God' are reversed*. The transgression of the first Adam is reversed by the obedience of the second Adam, and there comes into being the Head of a new humanity in the form of the Body of Christ which is the herald of the coming new creation.

Christ is not only a son of Adam as the Word made flesh He is also at one and the same time the Son of God. Genesis 5:3 indicates one of the meanings of the *imago Dei* of Genesis 1 is the relationship between a human father and a human son. 'When Adam had lived one hundred thirty years, he became the father of a son in his likeness, according to his image, and named him Seth.'

A similar relationship is indicated in the New Testament when Jesus is described by St Paul as the *eikon* or image of God (Col 1:15; 2 Cor 4:4). Christ shares a unique relationship with the Father as the true image and likeness of God; in his flesh he also shares a relationship with all humankind. He is the image and likeness of Adam, of sinful flesh. As Paul says in Romans 8:3, 'For God has done what the law, weakened by the flesh, could not do; by sending his own Son in the *likeness* of sinful flesh, and to deal with sin, he condemned sin in the flesh'.

Christ's unique being as the image and likeness of God and of human beings is for *the purpose of re-establishing human beings in their created purpose in relationship to God and each other*. So

141

Christ invites his disciples to enter into that unique relationship he shares with the Father by placing this name upon their lips in the prayer he gives them (Matt 6:9; cf Gal 4:6: 'God sent the Spirit of his Son into our hearts, crying, "Abba! Father!"').

This restoration of human communion with God and each other is identified with the person of Jesus Christ; the truth of the restored relationship between God and the creature inheres in the person of Jesus Christ. By his earthly obedience in the flesh he has minted out a new human being so that at every stage of our human development, from conception to death and beyond the grave, our relationship with God is set upon a new footing. This is the result of the presence in the world of the Son of God.

It is in the Holy Spirit that humans come to know and participate in the renewed truth of their relationship with God and each other as members of the Body of Christ in baptism. This Spirit is mediated by the risen Jesus Christ since he first received the Spirit, not for his own sake but for ours. As Son of God he did not need the Spirit in order to be one with God the Father; he is ever one with the Father and the Spirit. Yet he receives the Spirit. He is conceived by the Spirit in Mary's womb; he receives the Spirit in his baptism as the first act of his public ministry; he accomplishes his mighty works by the Spirit; he offers himself to the Father on the cross through the eternal Spirit (Heb 9:14); he is raised from the dead by the Spirit. Thus the ascended Christ unites his Body the church with himself by the Spirit in whom, once and for all, he sanctified our flesh. So those who are united with Christ are set on a way by which they are transformed and transfigured into his likeness. 'All of us, with unveiled faces, seeing the glory of the Lord as though reflected in a mirror, are being transformed into the same image from one degree of glory to another; for this comes from the Lord, the Spirit' (2 Cor 3:18).

The Critical Function of the Humanity of Jesus Christ in Expressing the Teleology of Human Existence

By his incarnation the Son of God minted out in our humanity the material basis of a renewed human being adapted to the truth of the relationships on which our humanity is grounded: our relationship to God and to each other. Jesus Christ in His person, is, the one place in the material universe of time and space where the truth of God's personal being is adapted by God's own action to the logical and verbal patterns of our human existence.

The basis of John Calvin's claim for the relationship between creation and redemption, allowing for the continuities and discontinuities presupposed by God's act of reconciliation, is the fact that God's relationship to the world is mediated in creation and redemption by the one Christ. The relationship God establishes with the creature relates to Christ and to the Spirit who 'accommodate' themselves in humility to the lowly estate of the creature, in order to raise it to God's glory. This being the case, *the created structures of human reason and experience become the means God uses to communicate God's self in acts of gracious union and communion.*[4]

This voluntary self-emptying of the Son of God is the basis of the reconstituting act whereby the obedience of the second Adam, in the humanity of Christ for our sake, replaces the wilful disobedience of the first Adam. Likewise, Calvin believes that Christ's humanity was not relinquished by his ascension. Christ did not need exaltation as the Son of God, for he is ever one with the Father and the Spirit. He was and is exalted for our sake. He never ceased to be God and to rule the universe, but he was exalted according to his manifestation for sinners as their High Priest.[5] God the Father has appointed Christ 'heir of all

---

4. See E D Willis, *Calvin's Catholic Christology: the Role of the So-Called 'extra Calvinisticum' in Calvin's Theology* (Leiden: E J Brill, 1966).
5. Calvin, *Institutes* 2 13 2, cf his *Commentary on Hebrews* (on 5:7).

things' (Heb 1:2) according to his accommodation to our lowliness, not according to his eternal divinity.

Calvin's use of what later became known as the *extra Calvinisticum* ensured that he was able to give theological significance to the relative ethical judgments that we are called upon to make as Christians and non-Christians, without compromising the free grace of the gospel. The relationship between God and the creature established in Christ takes account of the relativities of the human situation. This situation is mediated by the person of Jesus Christ who accommodates and continues to accommodate himself through the Holy Spirit to the created modes of our existence as the means whereby he wills to exercise his rule in the church and the world. The focus of theological coherence for Calvin is thus this-worldly and cosmic in its nature and scope.

In the light of the cosmic scope of the biblical witness to God's economy of salvation as fulfilled in Jesus Christ, it is clear that one cannot understand the relationship between the church and the world as involving two different realities, the 'sacred' and the 'secular'. There are not two realities but one which is defined by the action of God in God's self revelation in Jesus Christ. He it is who defines the nature of the church and the world in their relationship and difference, since he is both the creator Word and the incarnate Word who reconciles the world to God. He fulfils the divine purpose for creation.[6]

So the question for the church in the context of its life in the world is not whether but how it should witness in both word and deed to the truth of its life in Jesus Christ, as Lord of the church and of the world. The church's establishment of hospitals in the middle ages and its continued involvement in this form of health care indicates the Christian conviction that it is God's will to renew human beings in the context of the cosmic scope of God's reconciling purpose. Hospitals proclaim the church's commitment to this holy purpose of God; to renew

---

6. Cf D Bonhoeffer, *Ethics* (London: SCM, 1955), 55ff.

creation and safeguard it against all that is inimical to its created purpose.

The issue, then, is not whether the church should or should not be involved in serving the needs of people who are sick but whether the present way it performs this task is the most appropriate, given the needs of the community in which it is placed.

Secondly, the church must ask itself, and not simply from the point of view of efficiency, whether this task should be carried out in cooperation with other Christian churches. This question is of particular relevance to the Uniting Church of Australia which, according to its *Basis of Union*, has this mandate not as an accidental but essential characteristic of its life.

The 'Compassion' of God as a Basis for Christian Ethical Claims

This paper attempts to address some basic underlying assumptions of the *Interim Report on Sexuality* of the Uniting Church in Australia's Assembly Task Group on Sexuality.[1] The report contains much that is unexceptional and worthwhile as information for the church to consider in its life as the people of God. However, as will become obvious in this presentation, I contend that it is deeply flawed in its presentation of the basis of Christian ethical claims, in particular as these claims relate to the question of the report's advocacy of homosexual relationships being appropriately recognised and liturgically celebrated by the church (section 5 41). The basis for this advocacy is understood to be the recognition of people who are in a 'right relationship'. By a 'right' relationship the report has previously asserted that Christians should model their actions in relationship to one another on the action of God, in particular, the action of God in sending God's Son, Jesus Christ, into the world (4 3). 'Right' relationships then are those in which God's relationship to the world is 'modelled' (4 4); 'right' relationships 'are characterised by *agape*, the *love, caring* and the *compassion* embodied in Jesus Christ' (4 6).

Now the report states that in the church's consideration of sexuality, 'theological discourse has too often begun with the fall, rather than with the goodness of God's creation and the incarnation of Christ'.[2] Consequently, the Report seeks to understand the purpose of the act which it regards as central to its understanding of 'right relationships', the sending of God's Son into the world. This act is to be understood apart from the 'fall'. Now this claim is essentially wrong-headed.

---

1. *Interim Report on Sexuality*, Uniting Church in Australia, 1996.
2. *Interim Report on Sexuality*, Introduction, 8.

The purpose of God's action in sending the Son of God into the world to clothe himself with our humanity and to shed of his blood is precisely to deal with the consequences of the human race's fallenness. Of course, in this action of God in Christ God reaffirms the goodness of creation. But this affirmation is *in and through, not apart from, the fallenness of our common humanity* which Christ assumed. From the moment of his conception to his death, he sanctifies and heals this humanity in its relationship to God and our fellow human beings.

Gregory of Nazianzen, a bishop of Cappadocia, coined the well-known saying in this connection, 'the unassumed is the unredeemed'. By this he meant that the church understands the being of the human creature in relationship to God in the light of God's action in the incarnation of Christ. The fact that Christ became fully human entails that the totality of our humanity, our being who we are as humans before God and each other, is redeemed from the consequences of the fall by and in Jesus Christ. This is the basic assertion of the early creedal councils of the church in the fourth and fifth centuries. At the councils of Nicaea and Chalcedon it was declared against all the heresies which confronted the church that Jesus Christ is both *homoousios* with God and ourselves. That is, in the one person Jesus Christ is confessed to be both God and man. The purpose of these creedal affirmations is to safeguard the evangelical truth that in Jesus Christ God acts to re-create the creature in relationship to God and its fellows. This action of God is of such a nature that it effects the reconciliation of the world to God. It is both cosmic and eschatological in scope.

The purpose of this paper is to ask, in relation to the Report and its claims about ethical decision making, whether it is possible to use the idea of 'compassion', expressed by God's action in sending God's Son into the world, as a 'model' of 'right' relationships. When God's compassion is abstracted from the person of Jesus Christ and turned into an idea or 'model' of what constitutes 'right' human relationships, then the essential nature of God's redeeming action in Jesus Christ loses its focus and becomes translated into the general notion of 'mutual acceptance'. It is then concluded that if relationships between homosexual people are 'right', within the terms of the Report's peculiar definition of right relationships, then 'there are no legitimate reasons for rejecting homosexuality or homosexual relationships'. Because homosexual relationships can be classified as 'right', that is, showing care and compassion, it is asserted that the church should recognise and affirm such relationships.

In what follows we intend to show that such a view of 'compassion' as the basis of the church's ethical claims not only entails a distorted understanding of the biblical witness concerning the incarnation of God's Son. As a consequence it also fails to provide an adequate basis for any definition of what it is to be human in relationship with God and our fellows.

The noun for 'compassion' (*splanchnon*) in the New Testament denotes the 'seat of feelings or sensibilities', understood to be related to the inward parts of a person. The compound *asplanchnos* means 'cowardly' or having 'no guts'. The verb *splanchnizomai*, 'to have compassion', occurs in the New Testament only in the Synoptic Gospels, in three parables. The lord has compassion on the servant (Matt 18:27), the father has compassion on the prodigal (Luke 15:20), and the Samaritan has compassion on the man fallen among thieves (Luke 10:33). Elsewhere in the Synoptics the verb refers only to Jesus. It is he who shows compassion (see Mark 1:42; 6:34; 8:2; 9:22; Matt 9:36; 14:14; 20:34; cf Luke 7:13). In each case what is portrayed is not so much a human emotion as a messianic characterisation of the person of Jesus.

In Paul's writings only the plural noun *splachna* occurs. Introduced in very personal passages, it conveys a sense of the deepest emotions which unite the whole human person (see 2 Cor 6:11-12; 2 Cor 7:13ff, Philemon 7, 12 and 20). In Philippians 2:1 *splachna* denotes Christian affection, but it must be remembered that in the context of Philippians 1:8 the *splachna* as an affection moving the whole person is possible only 'in Christ'. The genitive 'of Christ' denotes the author.

Principally, then, where the verb 'to have compassion' occurs in the New Testament it refers to the person of Jesus Christ. It belongs to the relationship established between himself and people. 'When he saw the crowds, he had *compassion* for them, because they were harassed and helpless, like sheep without a shepherd' (Matt 9:36). 'When he went ashore, he saw a great crowd; and he had *compassion* for them and cured their sick' (Matt 14:14). 'When the Lord saw her, he had *compassion* for her and said to her, "Do not weep"' (Luke 7:13).

Now in all these examples the relationship Jesus establishes between himself and the crowd, the sick, and the widow, is one in which the need of the crowd or the person becomes transferred to Jesus. Their need becomes his; it modifies his inner being in a literal sense. It is this fact and its implications which must be understood when G Kittel maintains that the verb *splanchnizomai*, to have compassion, 'has messianic significance, for it is only Jesus who shows compassion in the synoptic gospels'.[3]

So to take up the meaning of the 'compassion of God' one has to start with drawing out the implications of precisely what is involved in Jesus having or showing compassion. The Christian tradition confesses that it is in the person of Jesus Christ that God is incarnate for the purpose of recreating humanity in relationship to God and in relationship to other human beings. It understands salvation to be grounded in the person of Jesus. He is worshipped as Lord, and it is presupposed that he mediates the relationship in which creation now finds itself as having a promised new being, since he who is to come is the one through whom all things were

---

3. G Kittel, *Theological Dictionary of the New Testament*, vol 1 (Grand Rapids: Eerdmans and Paternoster Press, 1985), 1067.

created. Christian salvation is cosmic in scope because the one in whom this salvation is grounded is the Creator Word of God.

We must therefore understand that Jesus 'having compassion' is related to the saving purpose of the incarnation of God. His compassion is the means by which he shows forth the manner of God's saving purpose. He takes to himself the neediness of the creature; he makes it his own by 'having compassion'. This entails that the configuration of God's action in Christ is determined from first to last by God's determination not to allow the creature's being to be engulfed by that which is inimical to its being in relationship to God's self. God takes to himself in Jesus that which negates and suffocates the creature's life in relationship to God. God in Christ takes responsibility for the creature in its relationship to God's self. He bears its burden of alienation and estrangement from God even to the depths of his own godforsakenness on the cross.

But Jesus' action of 'having compassion' is not to be understood as if he were simply a passive subject, absorbing the alienation of the human condition. In taking to himself the creature's alienation Jesus Christ not only bears the burden of estrangement from God. He recreates the creature, reconstitutes it as a creature. He not only justifies, he also sanctifies our humanity in relationship to God and in relationship to our fellow human beings. He therefore becomes and is the mediator of our relationship with God and of our relationship with each other.

Now the configuration of this action of God in Jesus Christ, as the fulfilment of the economy of salvation established by God's covenanted relationship with creation, is determined by the freely elected commitment of God to the creature. This commitment is presupposed in the creation of the world as a distinct entity, a creaturely reality in relationship with God. That is to say, God is so free in respect of God's own being that the existence of the creature, far from being a threat to the dominion and lordship of God, is established by God with a creaturely integrity and freedom that images God's own freedom and integrity as God. The grace of creation consists, therefore, in the fact that, according to Moltmann,

> God withdrew his eternity into himself in order to take time for his creation and to leave his creation its own particular time. Between God's essential eternity and the time of creation stands *God's time* for creation—the time appointed through his resolve to create.[4]

This act of God in creation presupposes in God the freedom to be for the other. This freedom to be for the other is not established by creation's relationship with God; otherwise, God would be dependent upon the existence of the creature in order to be God. To possess the capacity of being in freedom for the other, God as the Creator must presuppose in God's own being the freedom to be for the other. This is the ground of the unique Christian doctrine of God as a holy Trinity. The dogma of the Trinity is the church's reflection upon the freedom of God in the economy of salvation, fulfilled in Jesus Christ, to be both One and Another in the unity of a Third for the sake of the creature's creation and recreation in relationship to God. The distinctions in God of the persons, or the *hypostases,* are absolute distinctions, since they are grounded in God's determination to be who God is. Thus we must say that God's own life presupposes a freedom of persons who in absolute difference are in relationship. It is this act of relationship which constitutes the being of God as the one true God, Father, Son and Holy Spirit. This unity of God consisting as a being in communion has profound implications for the nature of the creature who is created by God for personal relationship with God.

In the action of becoming incarnate, God does not cease to be God by becoming that which is not God, a creature, in the person of Jesus Christ. God's becoming incarnate in Jesus Christ and the relationships established in the economy of salvation for the sake of the creatures' creation and recreation are not

---

4.   J Moltmann, *God in Creation* (London: SCM, 1985), 114.

simply a repetition of the relationships in which God exists in and for God's self. The relationship between what has been called the 'immanent' and 'economic' Trinity presupposes an ineffable condescension of God. This condescension of God has, as its purpose, not the revelation of a metaphysical mystery concerning the being of God's inner life, but the creation and recreation of the creature in relationship to God. The economy of salvation takes place not for the enrichment of God's being but for the sake of the creature, that it may participate as a creature in the glory of God's own life and love.

This can be expressed only in the language of worship, of doxology. In the language of worship, grounded as it is in the celebration of the events of the historical action of God in the economy of salvation, God is addressed in words which are offered in the form of confession, prayer and praise. These words refer to God in ways which pass human comprehension, since the words that are used presuppose, in their being predicated of God, the ineffable mystery of the voluntary condescension of God to create and recreate the creature.[5] For this very reason St Basil the Great enjoined his readers, that in considering the meaning of the dogma of the unity of God as three persons, 'dogma is to be observed in silence . . . The meaning of dogma is difficult of understanding for the very advantage of the reader'.[6]

---

5.   On this see W Pannenberg, 'Doxology and Analogy', in *Basic Questions in Theology*, vol 1 (London: SCM, 1970); E Schlink, 'The Structure of Dogmatic Statements as an Ecumenical Problem', in *The Coming Christ and the Coming Church* (Edinburgh: Oliver & Boyd, 1967).

6.   *De Spiritu Sancto* in *The Library of Nicene & Post Nicene Fathers,* vol viii, P Schaff & H Wace eds; see also D Bonhoeffer, *Christology* (London: SCM, 1966), 27: 'To speak of Christ means to keep silent; to be silent is to speak. The proclamation of Christ is the church speaking from a proper silence . . . We must study Christ in the humble silence of the worshipping community'.

7.   *Anselm: Basic Writings* (Lasalle, Illinois: Open Court, 1962).

As a preliminary reflection on the subject matter of this paper we may say that the compassion of God is not a characteristic of God considered as some abstract quality but is grounded in the manner in which God chooses to be God. God is one in the freely constituted relationships of God's being in which there is in God's own life a relationship of above and below, a sender and one who is sent. In God's own triune life there is distinction and relationship of persons in which absolute difference and absolute identity are constitutive of God's own eternal life. Such a view of God, as triune, is critical for an understanding of the nature of the creature in relationship to God.

This God does not cease to be who God is in becoming man in Jesus Christ. Thus the relationship which God establishes between God's self and the creature is congruent with the fact and the manner of who God is as God. Jesus' compassion for the creature is not simply a compassion for the creature in its dependency and frailty as a creature, created from the dust of the earth, but for a creature who in its creaturely frailty has become subject to the thraldom of sin and death. The greatness and the goodness of God is that God's compassion in Jesus Christ does not simply entail an action of God toward the creature in its created unlikeness to God. Rather, the incarnation of the Son of God is an act of condescension and identification with the creature in its being subject to the malignant claims of corruption and death. God's compassion is such as to take the neediness of the creature and make it God's own for the sake of the creature who is powerless before these negative claims. In this way we learn that the exercise of God's compassion, God's freedom to be with and for the other, as it finds expression in the incarnation of the Son of God, has as its purpose the reconstitution of the creature as a creature in relationship to God and its fellows.

The Bible understands this configuration of God's action by other means as well. We see the same pattern or order of God's being and action in the relationship between the law and the cult in the context of the covenant that God makes with Israel.

Here it is proclaimed that it is God's gracious purpose that the creature should be renewed in obedience to God, that this obedience, encompassing the creature's relationship to God and its fellows, would be translated into its flesh, its very existence. For example, Jeremiah 31:31-33 says,

> The days are surely coming, says the Lord, when I will make a new covenant with the house of Israel and the house of Judah. It will not be like the covenant that I made with their ancestors when I took them by the hand to bring them out of the land of Egypt—a covenant that they broke, though I was their husband, says the Lord. But this is the covenant that I will make with the house of Israel after those days, says the Lord: I will put my law within them, and I will write it on their hearts; and I will be their God, and they shall be my people.

Important for our understanding of the compassion of God is that this is specifically the manner in which the creature is reconstituted from within the structures of its creaturely being in relationship to God and its fellows. This means that the compassion of God cannot be considered to be an abstract quality of God's being but the specific configuration of God's action in the creation and recreation of the creature. It is in this respect that it may be understood to provide a basis of Christian ethical discourse, since it relates to *the renewal of the creature as a creature*. It thus specifies the truth concerning the creature's being by specifying the truth concerning the nature of the relationship between God and the creature that is renewed by God's action in the economy of salvation.

The configuration or the structure of God's compassionate action in Christ, who for the sake of the creature and in obedience to the Father wills to render his life up to death, presupposes the relationship between the Father and the Son. We come to theological knowledge of what the creature is in its relationship to God as this relationship is translated by Christ's vicarious obedience into the flesh of human being. This is the basis upon which the compassion of God is to be seen as the foundation of Christian ethical claims. For it is this action of God which specifies the truth concerning our creaturely being, expressing it in the paradoxical form as the truth concerning the untruth of creaturely being.

This way of understanding who the creature is in relationship to God may be seen in St Anselm's understanding of the necessity of Christ's incarnation in the *Cur Deus Homo* (*Why God Became Man*).[7] Anselm is at pains to point out that the truth of the creature which Christ assumes in its relationship to God, its teleology, the created trajectory of the creature's life, is re-established through the lived life of the incarnate Word. This lived life presupposes a voluntary and therefore an ineffable condescension on the part of the Son of God. 'At the heart of Cur Deus Homo there is not rational necessity but Divine Grace.'[8]

Karl Barth's stringently criticises St Anselm's rejection of the idea of God's freedom to forgive the creature by compassion alone. Anselm's argument derives from his recognition of the particular way in which God has dealt with humankind. In inestimable freedom God accommodates God's self to the created truth of the creature's relationship to God in order to re-establish it in the truth *as a creature*.[9]

For St Anselm the relationship between creaturely and divine truth was one which, though real, nevertheless involved the greatest disparity. This disparity is overcome by an act of will on the part of God the Word, in whom all things cohere. Anselm's emphasis on the voluntary nature of Christ's humiliation, the freely willed obedience of Christ in relation to his death, is intended to underline the fact that the divine and creaturely truths, while united by the ineffable condescension of

---

8.   J McIntyre, *St Anselm and His Critics* (Edinburgh: Oliver & Boyd, 1954), 193.

9.   See K Barth, *Church Dogmatics* 4/1 (Edinburgh: T&T Clark, 1956), 485ff.

Christ, are distinguished by the purposive teleology of Jesus' earthly life. Anselm's intention here is, on the one hand, to safeguard the actuality of the Son's humiliation as dependent upon God's free initiative. On the other hand, in the light of this initiative of grace, he wants to give full place to the actual obedience of Christ as a human being as the act in and through which God re-establishes the creature as a creature in relationship to God.

For St Anselm the only reality in which it was possible to conceive sin as having occurred is that of the creature in its wilful failure in obligation to the truth of its created being in relationship to God. God is obliged to no one. Consequently, if the creature's sin is to be removed the Son must freely assume the form of a human being. The element of judgment that Anselm sees in the atonement derives from the fact that sin could appear to be under no law or obligation, and therefore be like God, if the Son of God did not freely submit to judgment. God's justice and compassion are therefore seen to be one through the willed obedience and death of God's Son. What Anselm argues for is an understanding of the integral relationship between the incarnation and the atonement, since it is possible to understand the fulfilment of an obligation to the truth only as a free act of the creature *qua creature*.

The substance of St Anselm's argument is that the voluntary nature of the Son of God's condescension for the sake of the creature presupposes an infinite disparity between God's Supreme Truth and creaturely truth. Within this infinite disparity, the teleology, the willed purpose, the obedience of Jesus' human life establishes the freedom of the creature in relation to the Supreme Truth. Anselm therefore argues that if God were to forgive sin by compassion alone, it would entail ignoring the fact and the manner of Jesus' life of obedience. In such circumstances sin, which originates in and can only be predicated of creaturely being and truth would either be predicated of God or would remain unpunished and thus be shown to be like God—that is, under obligation to no one. This

Anselm rejects, primarily because this is not the way God has acted through the obedience of the Son of God as a man.

That Karl Barth signally fails to appreciate this point is shown by the way he deals with Anselm's argument which arises when Anselm's disciple asks him

> since God is free as to be subject to no law, and to the judgement of no one, and is so merciful as that nothing more merciful can be conceived, and nothing is right or fit save as he wills, it seems a strange thing for us to say that he is wholly unwilling or unable to put away an injury done to himself, where we are wont to apply to him for indulgence with regard to those offences which we commit against others.

Barth holds that Anselm

> thinks he can overcome this by saying that the freedom of God is inwardly conditioned by that *quod expedit aut quod decet, nec benignitas dicenda est, quae aliquid Deo indecens operatur.* (What is best and fitting should not be called compassion which does anything improper to the divine character.) A God who willed to lie would not be God. Nor would a God who willed to forgive without the prior fulfilment of this condition.[10]

The 'fittingness' of which St Anselm speaks is that of the way that God has actually taken in the act of atonement. The liberty of God and the creature is understood in terms of the way the Son of God has voluntarily assumed the creature's form for the creature's sake. That is why there is no liberty, *quod expedit aut quod decet* ('as regards what is best or fitting'), precisely because

---

10.   *Ibid,* 486; see St Anselm, *Cur Deus Homo* Book 1 (Lasalle, Illinois: Open Court, 1962), ch xii, 204-205; G Watson, 'Karl Barth and St Anselm's Theological Program', *Scottish Journal of Theology* 30, 1977: 31-45 and 'A Study in St Anselm's Soteriology and Karl Barth's Theological Method', *Scottish Journal of Theology* 42, 1989: 493-512 (both in this volume).

it is through the person of Jesus that God is obedient. Since this in fact is how the matter stands in terms of the relationships and differences between the supreme truth of God and contingent creaturely truth, it is impossible to say that God can lie, that is, act as though sin were subject to no law and like God was obliged to no one.[11]

The basis of this impossibility is not an abstract theory about what God can or cannot do. To say that God cannot lie is therefore the same as saying, in the context of St Anselm's argument, that the Son of God became truly human for the sake of our redemption. It is on this basis that Anselm proves the necessity of Christ's death and thus explains God's action in creation and redemption.

This excursus into St Anselm's understanding of the centrality of Jesus' freely offered human obedience is intended to reinforce the view, previously established. The 'compassion' of God must be based upon and configured by the action of God who in freedom condescends to accommodate God's self to the contingent relationship in which the creature exists before God: the God/creature relationship being re-established in its created integrity by God's personal action; the obedient Son in relationship to the Father and the Spirit. Otherwise, as Barth's criticism of St Anselm shows, the idea of God's compassion will be defined in terms of an abstract notion of God's freedom or, as is more likely to be the case today, as an idea of the possibilities inherent in the human capacity for love and 'right relationships'.

The revelation of God's compassion indicates that the creature's relationship to God has a specific configuration. Consequently the creature, as illumined by this act, has a specific nature or created purpose. It is to explicate the form of this being illumined by God's action to which we now turn. In what follows it is my intention to show how this 'compassion' of God, as defined above, may be seen as the basis of Christian

---

11.   Anselm, *Cur Deus Homo*, Book 1, ch xii, 205f.

ethical claims, in so far as these claims verify the truth of the creature whom God has taken to God's self in the humanity of God's Son.

We have argued that the compassion of God cannot be understood as an abstract notion of God's beneficence. God's compassion must be understood as grounded in the particular action of God's condescension and accommodation to the creature in the humanity of Jesus Christ, such particular action being configured by the relational being of God's triune life.

It is now my intention to argue that the particularity of God's act of compassion, in and by which the creature is reconstituted as a creature in relationship to God and other creatures, reveals human being, configured by God's act of creation and re-creation, to have a particular ontological structure. Human being is shown by God's action in Christ to be fundamentally relational. It is relational in terms of its created nature as male and female, and such relationality has as its purpose the eschatological vocation of all creaturely being—the perfection of all creation in the relationship between Christ and his church. It is the relationship between Christ and his church, grounded in the incarnate obedience of the Son to the Father's purpose and realised in the Spirit in the creation of the church as Christ's body, that the created purpose of human beings is revealed.

The view espoused in the Assembly's Sexuality Task Group Report is that the relationships in the Christian *koinonia* must be understood in terms of *each individual's self understanding*. That is, who human beings are in relationship to God and their fellow human beings is to be understood as grounded in the individual's perceived sexual orientation. That such relationships as are established by individuals on the basis of their self-understanding must be recognised in and by the church with a mutuality of understanding which expresses 'compassion'. 'Compassion' is here understood in terms of mutual acceptance, since the love of Christ in which the

Christian *koinonia* subsists is characterised by unconditional acceptance.

But, on the basis of what has been said above, such a view of human being, created and reconciled to God in Jesus Christ, fails to bring to expression the truth of human being in relationship to God and to other human beings. It does this in at least three important respects.

Firstly, it fails to take account of the fact that the 'compassion' of God, which is the stated basis of the idea of unconditional acceptance, is grounded in the absolute differences and absolute unity of the relational being of God, the Father, the Son and the Holy Spirit. It fails to see that this fact has definite implications for the ontological configuration of the creature in relationship to God.

Secondly, the condescension of God grounded in God's 'compassion', at great cost recreates the creature as a creature; it establishes the truth of the creature in relationship to God and to its fellows precisely because God's being as compassionate entails God's freedom to be with and for the other. In encompassing this difference between the Creator and the creature God does not cease to be who God is in and for God's self as Father, Son and Holy Spirit. In fact, it is precisely as such that God in Christ re-establishes the relationship between God and the creature.

Thirdly, this act of recreation of the creature as a creature in relationship to God and its fellows involves those aspects of judgment and grace which, as we have indicated, were vital for St Anselm's insistence that God in Christ *does not forgive sin by compassion alone*. The purposive teleology of Jesus' life, His freely willed obedience to the Father fulfilled in the cross, re-establishes the creature as a creature in its created integrity. To ignore this configuration of Jesus' life of obedience fulfilled in the cross would entail that sin, which originates in and can only be predicated of creaturely being and truth, would either be predicated of God or would remain unpunished and thus appear to be like God—under obligation to no law. This St

Anselm rejected, primarily because this is not the way God has acted through the obedience of the Son of God as a Man.

In respect of the Report of the Task Group on Sexuality, one must say that the idea of *compassion* that is there presupposed as the basis for Christian ethical behaviour is shown to be fundamentally flawed. It fails to take into account the structure of the God/creature relationship revealed in Christ as both judged and renewed in the relationship between Christ and the church. It also fails to see that this relationship is at once the basis of Christian ethical claims as it re-establishes the creature in its created integrity as male and female in relationship to God and other creatures.

The discussion of the issue of homosexuality among Christians has been generally in terms of what is understood by 'sexuality', and focuses especially on either homo- and/or hetero-sexuality. It must be said that considerable progress has been made in the church and in society's dealing with issues associated with sexuality. This progress should not be over-looked in any discussion of the issue of homosexuality.[12]

'Progress' in my view is to be seen in the decriminalisation of consenting homosexual behaviour. The opponents of such decriminalisation usually put forward the view that decriminalisation implies acceptance of homosexuality in general. But decriminalisation does not imply acceptance of homosexuality; it is a first step in removing harsh, punitive attitudes towards this kind of behaviour by the state.

Secondly, there has been progress in the church pastoral attitudes towards homosexual people. The church has come to the view that homosexuals should be understood not judgmentally but as people to whom Christians should relate lovingly and responsibly. Some have seen the logical consequence of such a view as the sanctioning of those living in

---

12. I am indebted to the following article for some of the material in what follows: H Turner, 'Gender and Homosexuality', *Evangelical Review of Theology* 19/1, 1995: 43ff.

homosexual relationships as eligible for church membership, and thus eligible for ordination to its ministries. This view sees the changed attitude in the churches as the 'normalisation' of homosexuality. But this new attitude to homosexuality is no more or less than a fully Christian approach to this issue, as to any other aspect of human behaviour. It is a quite different matter to use such factors as decriminalisation and enlightened pastoral attitudes to reclassify homosexuality as an acceptable sexual norm.

There are many who are able to accept decriminalisation of homosexuality and genuinely support a more positive approach to homosexual people, but are left with little more than an inarticulate feeling that the public acceptance of homosexuals into the Christian ministry is not 'right'. A weakness in this view of ethical behaviour for and amongst Christians is that there is no agreed basis for public ethical claims in our culture. Ethics is said to derive from changing 'cultural values' and in a pluralist society we enter 'a night in which all cats are grey'. Ethics, issues of right and wrong, is reduced to matters of personal opinion—my lifestyle alongside yours. Such arguments are invoked to support a variety of sexual orientations as equally 'right' for different people. The church, too, imbibes this view from the culture in which it is immersed. This makes the task of presenting a view which seeks to counter such morés in terms of the faith of the church especially difficult.

On the basis of what we have argued concerning the theological meaning of God's compassion, we may say that the way in which it is configured by the nature of God, revealed in the relationship between God and the creature established in the person of Jesus Christ, will entail the following implications for the way in which human sexuality is considered in the context of the church.

The particular configuration of the creature's being, its relationality as the image of God in terms of the gender relationship, has Christological and consequently ecclesiological implications. Genesis 1:26-27 states that God makes humans in God's image by creating them male and female. This again is emphasised in 5:1-2.

> This is the list of the descendants of Adam. When God created humankind, he made them in the likeness of God. Male and female he created them, and he blessed them and named them 'Humankind' when they were created.

Here likeness to God is not spelled out in terms of the human creature's rationality, creativity, moral consciousness, free will or any other distinctive feature that distinguishes humans from animals. It is the fact of gender which affirms human beings in their created likeness to God; their humanness consists in the relationship presupposed by it.

Whereas the world of animals is 'created according to its' kind' or species, humankind is not so classified into various species of race or culture, but simply by way of gender. Gender is not a species; it is in their co-existence as male and female that their likeness to God, the basic form of their humanity, consists.

Neither is gender to be thought of as primarily identified with sexuality. The question of human reproduction is not mentioned until further on in the narratives of Genesis. Sexuality is basic to gender, but gender itself has a wider connotation and is that which, as a 'given', defines the human 'as in relationship with the other' in its relationship to God. Here it is not a question simply of relationship *per se* being the basis of the creature being in the image of God, but of the specific relationship of gender, maleness and femaleness.

It is an implication of this view that arguments for legitimating homosexuality as a complementary Christian life style or sexual orientation in fact break the co-humanity of the human species as male and female, and create another species called homosexual.

As John Zizioulas has made plain,[13] the basic vocation of human beings in their co-humanity as male and female is ecclesial; they image the relationship of Christ with the church. The real image of God of which the creature as male and female is the image is the relationship established by God in Christ's relationship to the church as His Body. The creature's humanity has this basic ecclesial orientation. The 'compassion' of God has this particular configuration since God in Christ recreates the creature in its created integrity by accommodating God's self to the creature's being in relationship to God, and incorporates them as members of his body. This has eschatological implications for the future of creation (Col 1:15ff; cf Eph. 1:3ff).

The homosexual relationship cannot in principle be an image of such a compassionate relationship as is established by God in Christ's relationship with the church, since it presupposes a relationship of *like to like* (ie, *homo*). The relationship of Christ to the church is not one of *like to like*; the *likeness* between Christ and the Church is one created out of great unlikeness by the free condescension of God's *compassion*. Such likeness as exists is not simply between God and the creature, but between God and the creature in its estrangement from God. It is the likeness in unlikeness of the gender relationship, of male and female, which establishes this as the relationship in which the creature exists as the human image of the God of 'unspeakable grace', to use Charles Wesley's memorable words.[14] But the homosexual relationship contradicts this likeness and therefore God's 'compassion' and creation's purpose.

On the basis of what has been argued concerning the manner of God's condescension in Jesus Christ, and the centrality of the human obedience of Jesus in considering the way in which the being of the creature is re-constituted by God's action, we may say that this ecclesial vocation of humanity mitigates against the

---

13. *Being as Communion* (New York: St Vladimir's Seminary Press, 1985).
14. Methodist Hymn Book, No 66 v 3.

church accepting the idea that homosexuality is a legitimate human expression of sexuality. It is therefore theologically untenable to present homosexuality as an equally valid alternative to the Christian and biblical view of the nature of humanity as created and re-created in the image of God by the vicarious obedience of the Son of God in fulfilling the Father's purpose for creation.

The 'compassion' of God, understood from the point of view of its strict trinitarian content, indicates that the Christian community is not free to redefine humanity without considering the theological implications of the gender relationship as indicating what it is to be human: made in the image of God.

Disablement in the Context of a Christian View of Creation

The context in which we consider the relationship between the existence of pain and disease—of disablement—and the Christian view of the nature of the human person as part of God's good creation, mitigates against the latter being understood as having any relevance. This is a consequence of the fact that the movement in sixteenth century European thought known as the Enlightenment, and its consequences, largely conditions the contemporary cultural context of the church.

A major consequence has been the creation of a mental world with which we become familiar before we can articulate its meaning. It is a world in which the 'knowing subject' defines external reality in terms of 'objective facts'. These 'objective facts' are 'value free', since they are the same for every reasonable person. These 'facts' are understood to be the determinate of truth. With unprecedented zeal the Enlightenment proposed to explain the world as something that is without purpose. The idea of purpose, as of any other 'value', is understood to belong to the 'subjective' sphere and is to be excluded as a determinate of truth on the precise ground of it being a subjective variable. This dichotomy between fact and value, the explanation of everything in terms of antecedent causes according to a mechanistic model of reality, and the relegation of values to the privatised sphere of the individual subject is the Enlightenment's most characteristic and influential legacy. With characteristic zeal the Enlightenment thinkers pursued the idea of the methodological elimination of purpose from the study of the human, to the extent that it is assumed in our culture to be a universally valid maxim. From this disembodied position everything else, whether persons or things, are useable and or discardable. As Colin Gunton points out in his excellent book, *The One, The Three and the Many*,[1] 'modernity is characterised by a philosophy of non-relation, of disengagement, in which human subjects, standing apart from each other and the world, use each other and the world as instruments'.

The world we inhabit is pervasively influenced by the 'modern' worldview which derives from the Enlightenment. Reality is what can be defined by our measurement of it. The material world can be described accurately by us in terms of models which are basically mechanical and mathematical. The reality of the other person is less real than our own mind and thought.

The dominant view of our culture is that *we* are the world; we 'absorb' the world and give it meaning at the expense of community and the natural environment. Postmodernism in its critique of modernity came to prominence as a consequence of its recognition that the world as it is in itself, the world apart from our description of it, is inaccessible to human beings. Thus the schools of postmodernity view language, to all intents and purposes, as the only reality. The attempt is made to shift attention from study of the world as an objective entity to the study of texts and the various cultural linguistic realities which make up the world. The world is not *the* world but a multitude of small textual worlds, the linguistic worlds in which we live and move and have our being. Thus there is no such thing as the truth. There is merely this truth or that truth according to the operating context; there is my truth and your truth. All we have recourse to is a shifting sea of relativities none of whose views can be compared critically.

The problem with such views purveyed by some postmodern critics of modernity is that the claims they make presuppose the very God's eye view of 'truth'/'reality', of which they are so critical and which they intend to refute with

---

1. Cambridge: Cambridge University Press, 1993, 12.

their account of language. It is a classic example of the famous Cretan saying, 'All Cretans are liars'.

In terms of the claims made implicitly and explicitly by Christians with respect to God's relationship to the world, to be self-consistent Christianity must take Jesus Christ as the human expression of God's reality and truth. This seemingly imperialist claim on the part of Christians is simply a way of expressing the fact that in any particular culture what is most real, what is important, will be defined by what is taken to be the basis of life's meaning.[2] It is what defines the public culture and the issues of the public agenda which are seen to be important. It articulates a view that 'absorbs' the world. The question is, then, what is this Christian perspective which 'absorbs' the world and gives meaning to the painful questions of disease, suffering and disability in their multifarious manifestations?

It is important to emphasise this question in the context of a culture in which the predominant views are alien to the Christian faith's presuppositions. These are that human life has a characteristic unity and purpose which establish who we are as persons in relationship to God and each other. This unity is not a creation of the human mind or an arbitrary choice of some group interest, but derives from the nature of Christ and the Spirit as God's personal presence with and for the creature, in creation, reconciliation and promised redemption.

The Church's Understanding of the World

The biblical view that this world with all its creatures is a creation that is derived from the historical experience of Israel. Historically, the Pentateuch received its present form only after the eighth century prophets. The basis of their word to the people of Israel was God's election of Israel expressed in the

---

2.   See Sue Patterson, *Realist Christian Theology in a Postmodern Age* (Cambridge: Cambridge University Press, 1999).

covenanted relationship. This relationship was constitutive of Israel's being as a people; it was the meaning of the existence of the world and its peoples.

Israel believed that the way God had acted in relationship to it was also true of God's relationship to the world. Hence, in the creation accounts of Genesis God leads the world out of the threatening watery chaos, as God led Israel. God brings forth the dry land as a cosmos, giving it to humans as their habitation, in the same manner that God gave the land of Canaan to God's people as their home. Stamped by their saving experience of God through their exodus from Egypt and the gift of the land, Israel's understanding of the world as God's creation entailed that they saw the world not as a self enclosed series of random events featuring an eternal cycle of ultimate meaninglessness. On the contrary, just as they understood their history to be guided by God's redemptive purpose, so also the world had a history, a purpose. Consequently, the Israelites historicised the creation myths which they borrowed from their cultural and ethnic neighbours; they turned them into accounts which related not abstract and timeless ideas, but the history of the world and Israel's place as God's people in that world.

God's presence and activity in the world, as in relationship to Israel, is one which preserves its being and safeguards it against a return to primeval chaos, the disorder over which God triumphed in the beginning. God preserves Israel and safeguards it as God's people from the threat of annihilation by natural catastrophes such as the desiccating wilderness and the flood. Similarly, the powers of negation and death, signified by sickness, which reach into the life of the world are reminders of the fragility of the world's existence, dependent every moment that it exists on God's gracious care.

But the faith of Israel expressed in the writings of the Old Testament does not merely testify to the Exodus experience and the consequent faith in God as the Creator of the world. It also witnesses to the hope of a future in which creation will be renewed by God's action. This will reveal the final triumph of

God over all that is inimical to God's purposes and therefore negates the life of God's creature. Many of the Psalms make this point clear, and the Book of Job emphasises it.

While this vision of a renewed creation echoes the experience of the initial exodus from Egypt, it goes beyond simply recalling that fact. Isaiah 48:21 says that those who go out in freedom will neither hunger nor thirst: their path is easy because all barriers have been cleared away. Nature itself will participate in this future liberation of God's people (49:11). The mountains will break forth into rejoicing and the trees will clap their hands (49:13; 55:12). Waters will spring forth in the wilderness and streams in the desert (35:6). All nations will see this and know that the God of Israel is the God of their salvation (41:11; cf 42:17; 45:14ff). This eschatological vision fulfils the original creation. The exodus out of the chaos of slavery and the present world existing under the threat of chaos, preserved by God's providential care from the waters above the firmament and the encroaching threat of the sea, will be followed by the transfiguration of creation in the unveiled presence of God.

It was Israel's understanding of itself as called and chosen by God through its particular historical experience that made it recognise its gracious God as the Creator of the world. Israel's experience of God has important implication for our understanding of the nature of created reality. The world created by God in freedom is not simply a contingent entity, but is made to be the sphere in which God can establish a personal relationship with the creature. Thus the being of the world is one in which the personal relationship willed by God with the creature has priority over the impersonal. The Bible sees human dignity and worth grounded in a relationship established by God with human beings prior to and independent of any human action. Although this relationship is corrupted by human sin, it is upheld and confirmed by God's action in both judgment and grace.

The Implications of the Biblical View of the World as Created

To know the God of Israel is to know that one's own existence and that of the world is created for relationship with the other: with God and other human beings. This is the fundamental grammar of creation, and it is seen already in the covenant established between God and Israel.

The Christian conviction is that Jesus is the Christ, the Messiah of Israel. As the New Covenant he fulfils the covenanted relationship of God with Israel for all humanity. This entails that the church took over the view of God's relationship with the world as its Creator that is found in the Old Testament. The church saw itself as the inheritor of Israel's faith. The incarnation of Jesus Christ is the actual intersection of our creaturely being and life in time and space by the eternal being and life of the person of the Son of God. He thus constitutes himself as the place in space and time where God's own life is accommodated to the structures of created nature. His being is the means by which the intelligibility of creation, its created being and life, is established and re-established in both its contingent and purposeful relationship with God.

The church's being created as the earthly Body of this heavenly Head precipitates it in a movement of mission in and towards the world. The relationship between the life of the church and its mission in the world, as it presses towards the fulfilment of all things in Christ, is not created or sustained by the church but is given to it. The church exists in this relationship to the world because of what it is in Jesus Christ. Its actions in the world in the name of Christ testify to the Lordship of the one in whom the world finds its true being. The 'cosmic' dimension of the church's mission is not an accidental characteristic, but is of the essence of its mission. That the church has thus become involved in a ministry of healing indicates that it understands that the one in whom its life is sustained is involved in an ongoing confrontation with those powers of negation which threaten and distort the purpose of God's creation.

The New Testament uses at least two words to describe the action of healing. The verb hygiaino, to be healthy, is used in such passages as Luke 7:10 to describe the result of Jesus' action in healing someone ('When those who had been sent returned to the house, they found the slave in good health'). The adjective sozo means hale, sound, healthy; from it comes the English word hygiene. The other word used in connection with healing and health, with soundness or wholeness of body and mind, is the word σωζω, which means to save or rescue, to preserve unharmed. For example, Matthew 8:25 uses the word in the sense of preserving from harm. In the midst of a storm at sea the disciples in a boat cry out, 'Lord, save us! We are perishing!' The same word is used by St Paul in 1 Corinthians 1:21 to describe God's act of salvation by faith in Christ as the crucified Lord. 'For since, in the wisdom of God, the world did not know God through wisdom, God decided, through the foolishness of our proclamation, to save those who believe.'

The connection is made here between God's action in the world in Jesus Christ and the wholeness of human beings. The question for theology concerning people who are disabled is that healing and health is directly related to the relationship they have with God as God's creatures.

Implications of the Reformed View of the Relationship Between the 'Fall' and the Disorder Apparent in the Human Condition

The view taken by the Reformers of the sixteenth century was that the Genesis accounts of creation are historical as distinct from being mere fables. They are historical in the sense that God instituted a personal relationship with the human creature, and that such a relationship is determinative for understanding who the human creature is in relationship to God and other creatures. The Reformers knew that the human creature was created from the dust of the earth like all other creatures. It was different from other creatures not because it was created from different dust, but because God chose to relate to the human creature in a specific personal manner. They did not base their idea of the creation of human beings on some particular interpretation of sixteenth century science, whatever that may have been. (Although some, like the Lutheran Osiander, were active in publicising the views of Copernicus and the new science of astronomy.) Their view of the historicity of the creation of human beings was based on the fact that God chose to become a particular human being in order to recreate creation. The human being recreated by God in Jesus Christ is one who, *prior to Christ's incarnation*, was created for the purpose of personal communion with the Creator. This purpose was frustrated by human beings 'falling' away from God by their own choice; and this choice affects the physical and spiritual being of human persons. Since all humans are inter-related to each other by virtue of their creation, what happens in one affects all. The solidarity of the human family in 'fallenness' is a corollary of people being recreated in the humanity of Jesus Christ. It is the particular and historical nature of God's act of redemption of human beings in Christ that forms the basis of the Reformers' view that Adam was a 'historical' person—not some preconceived notion that the book of Genesis is a text book of palaeontology or biology. The incarnation of God presupposes that human beings are in a particular, but not to say unique, relationship with God; it is this conviction that makes Adam 'historical' and his 'fall' an existential reality of the human condition.

It is the historicity of the act of God's reconciliation of the creature which is the basis of the Reformed Christian's view of the historicity of the account dealing with the creation of human beings. To want to label this view as 'creationist' is naive. It is, more importantly, wrong in terms of the facts. What 'creationists' maintain is that the book of Genesis is somehow a 'scientific' textbook of the history of the world that this can be demonstrated by 'scientific' means. The Bible makes no such claim, nor do the Reformers.

What are the implications, for understanding the world, of this view of creation based on the understanding of the particularity of God's act of reconciliation as revealed in the life death and resurrection of the Son of God, Jesus the Christ?

By the incarnation of the Son of God the Christian faith understands that at a particular point in the space/time continuum God became a human being—a man, Jewish flesh assumed from the Virgin Mary. As both God from God and man born of a woman, Jesus Christ is the mediator between God and humankind. He ministers the things of God to humanity and the things of humanity, including our alienation, our fallenness, to God.

Our human nature understood in this context is shown to have its ground in Christ through whom creation itself came to be (John 1:1). For he is the basis of creation's rational order. His incarnation is the reconstitution of creation in its created relationship with God. In considering the question of disablement it cannot be without significance that Jesus Christ actually healed people of physical and spiritual disability. He took the side of the threatened and endangered creature against all that is inimical to its purpose, thus defending at the same time the glory of God the Creator (see Matthew 4:24; 8:16; 12:22; Mark 5:29; Luke 4:40). By his being and actions Jesus Christ recreates human beings in relationship with God and others at every stage of human development, from conception to death, and beyond death.

Such a theological context does not prescribe what ethical decisions Christians should make. But it does establish that human beings cannot be considered merely in terms of their biochemical, genetic make up. The situation of the embryo in the womb or the aged person cannot be described without reference to the ground of their being in Christ. It is the action of God in creation and reconciliation which both defines and sustains human beings in such a manner as to include a relationship with God at every stage of their physical and spiritual existence as persons created in the image of God.

This view has consequences for understanding the church's mission, since Christ's act of reconciliation and promised redemption is cosmic in scope. The 'new creation' which the New Testament church expectantly awaits is the fulfilment of Christ's reconciling purpose. This reconciling purpose is grounded in the whole trajectory of Jesus' life as the incarnate Son of God. It entails thinking of this act in terms of Jesus' whole life, death and resurrection, as he passes through every stage of human development. There takes place in him a reconstitution or recreation of our human being in relationship to God. God in Christ recreates the relationship between God's self and the creature in such a manner that it is not something that takes place, as it were, above our heads in some external way. Rather, God penetrates to the depths of our human condition and bears in God's own self the cost of our redemption. Consequently, the mission of the church has as an essential characteristic the healing of people's bodies and minds in the name of Christ the Saviour.

This, of course, does not happen by means of some forensic conjuring trick. Jesus, as God's own Son, bears in himself the pain of the godforsakenness of the human condition. From the first act of his public ministry there is marked out the way of the cross and resurrection. Through his obedient penitence in behalf of sinners and his healing he identifies with the diseased humanity which clung to him at every turn. He presses his way forward to the goal of his life, and embraces the cross as his life's fulfilment (cf Hebrews 2:10-17; 5:7-9).

The church's life in Christ must be considered not as something external to who Jesus Christ is for our sake; it is identical with what he wills to be for us. This means that the church cannot be a holy society dedicated to perpetuating the memory of a great religious teacher, but that it exists as a community 'in Christ' (cf 2 Corinthians 5:17; Gal 3:26; 5:6; Ephesians 2:10; Colossians 1:4; 1:24; 1Thessolonians 4:16;

Hebrews 3:14). The church's life inheres in the person of Jesus Christ, the Son of God. Thus the relationship between God and those who are disabled is not established by us but for us, by God's reconstitution of our human being in relationship to God's own self and in our relationship to each other in the community of the church as Christ's Body. As has been emphasised, this fact has important consequences for understanding ourselves in relationship to those who are disabled. These relationships can be understood only in the context of our being set on a path towards the renewal of our humanity which has taken place in Christ and is promised as the future of creation in him (Romans 8:19ff; 2 Corinthians 5:17; Revelation 21:1-4).

Euthanasia and the Incarnation of the Son of God in the Light of the *Basis of Union* of the Uniting Church

In his book *A Community of Character: Towards a Constructive Christian Social Ethic*,[1] Stanley Hauerwas calls attention to a critical factor for Christians making up their minds on attitudes to ethical issues which affect their life. He indicates that the accepted wisdom concerning ethical reflection is that analysis concentrates on 'problems', situations in which it is hard to know what to do. In such a context ethics is understood as a procedure for making decisions, resolving conflict of choice situations.

This account of ethics and ethical decision making as concerning 'problems' suggests that ethics can be construed as a rational science that evaluates alternative solutions. It is assumed that moral decisions should be based on rational principles about which there is general agreement, and are not directly related to any one set of beliefs or convictions. Ethics then can be seen and practised as a branch of decision making science, and taught as a disinterested social science.

The problems associated with this standard account of moral reasoning are largely not apparent, though it has become the standard fare by which church councils and committees make their pronouncements on this or that ethical question. But the standard account poses critical questions for the Christian community's understanding of the ethical issues which affect its life and relationships with the structures and cultures of the societies in which it is placed. For from the perspective of the standard account such things as beliefs, dispositions, and above

---

1.   Notre Dame Ind: University of Notre Dame Press, 1981.

all character, cannot be the subject of rational thought and are therefore mostly irrelevant to the meaning of ethical discourse. They are subjective variants which need to be isolated from the process of ethical decision making.

One only needs to state the implications of the standard account of ethical reasoning to see that it is quite inadequate as a vehicle for expressing the views on ethical issues of the Christian community. For it is basically those factors excluded by the standard account which, from the point of view of the Christian community, determine what kind of moral considerations, what 'reasons', count and the relative weight we give them in making moral judgments. This may mean that Christian ethics, instead of making Christians functional within the framework of pluralist liberal democracies of the West, will make them dysfunctional.

The following contends for the view that the Christian church must not allow its thinking and speaking on these important issues to be determined by the presuppositions of the culture in which it finds itself at any particular time. It must speak out of the truth of God which is the basis of its life in Christ, and do so in the light of the church's reflection on the meaning of this truth over the centuries.

We see this influence, however remarkable it may seem, in paragraphs 3 to 8 of the *Basis of Union of the Uniting Church in Australia* which deal with the central questions of the church, namely, its faith and unity, its nature, the Bible, the sacraments. In these paragraphs it is said that the UCA 'acknowledges' thus and thus. By so doing the church says that, although its knowledge of God and God's will does not come about without our work, it does not come about through it.

In paragraphs 3-8, 11, 15, 17 it is stated that the Uniting Church 'acknowledges' something or someone. For example, it is stated in paragraph 3 that the unity of the church is 'acknowledged' to be built upon the unity of 'the one Lord Jesus Christ'. The two propositions—one concerning the unity of God's people as the church and the other concerning the oneness or unity of Jesus Christ—presuppose an unexpressed condition. These statements assume that the coherence of their theological truth derives from and is addressed to the God before whom the statements are made. They presuppose the setting of theology in the context of prayer and worship.

This logical discrepancy is to be emphasised at all costs if we are to understand the intention of the theological statements contained in these important paragraphs of the *Basis of Union*. Dr J Davis McCaughey, first President of the Uniting Church, in his commentary on the *Basis of Union of the Uniting Church*,[2] maintains that paragraph 3

> is the most fundamental paragraph in the whole Basis. More than ever each phrase calls for serious reflection for it points beyond itself to the One to whom we belong and to some of the consequences of belonging to him . . . there is commitment by the Uniting Church present in every paragraph . . . In this paragraph it is stated unequivocally that the faith of the Holy Catholic and Apostolic Church is not a series of human aspirations: it is built upon Jesus Christ.

The paragraph in question begins in the following way,

> The Uniting Church acknowledges that the faith and unity of the Holy Catholic and Apostolic Church are built upon the one Lord Jesus Christ. The Church preaches Christ the risen crucified One and confesses him as Lord to the glory of God the Father. In Jesus Christ God was reconciling the world to himself. In love for the world, God gave his Son to take away the world's sin.

By the incarnation of the Son of God the tradition of the Christian faith understands that at a particular point in the space\time continuum God became a human being—a man, Jewish flesh assumed from the Virgin Mary. As both God from

---

2. *Commentary on The Basis of Union of the Uniting Church in Australia*, 19.

God and Man born of a woman, Jesus Christ is the Mediator between God and humankind. He ministers the things of God to humanity and the things of humanity, including our alienation, our fallenness, to God.

The Son of God in becoming a human did not cease to be God. Consequently our language and thought fulfil their intention in speaking of God when they terminate on Him. God, who exists beyond the spatio-temporal relationship established in Christ with the world, is nevertheless free to become what God is not in order to relate to the creature. In Christ God accommodates God's self to the world that is created out of nothing. God *'becomes'*, participates in a *coming into being* ('The word became flesh', John 1:14). Our this-worldly language in referring to God, on the basis of God's act of condescension in the Son of God, must take into account God's voluntary condescension to the creature. By this means our speaking of God, with our this-worldly language, points beyond itself to the transcendent ground of its truth in Christ.[3]

To take an example which relates directly to the question of the nature of humanity in relation to God: the fact of our existence in time and space. This is a fundamental structure of human existence. When the church reflected on this issue it was confronted in the culture in which it lived with radically different views than that which was presupposed by the incarnation of God in Christ. Greek/Roman thought tended in two directions in its speech about God, either as materialism in the Atomists and Lucretius or that God is detached and unknowable, leading to a mystical non-rational communion in the Platonic and Neoplatonic tradition. The concept of space/time which presupposed this tradition saw space and time as an infinite receptacle independent of what went on in it.

---

3.   On the following see T F Torrance, *Transformation and Convergence in the Frame of Knowledge* (Grand Rapids: Eerdmans, 1984); *Space, Time and Incarnation* (London: Oxford University Press, 1968); *Space, Time and Resurrection* (Edinburgh: Handsel Press, 1976).

From Renaissance sources Isaac Newton took up this idea and gave space and time an absolute status independent of the material bodies which it contained. Its role in Newton's system was to make natural objects determinate and thus knowable. But God could not be understood as contained by anything, therefore God could not be described in terms of space and time. God was the Container who contained the container of space/time. Newtonian physics was a powerful confirmation of the prevailing Deist theology of the eighteenth century which understood God as having only an indirect relationship to the world. It also provided the philosophical basis for the 19th century notion of the world as a closed system of mechanistic causality.

The early church, principally the Greek Fathers, rejected the view of space/time which they found in the prevailing culture. In St Athanasius' confrontation with the archheretic Arius we see the clash of these two views of reality. Arius denied that we can speak of God in this-worldly terms; to do so would be to make God a creature. Since there was once when God was not a Father, Jesus could not be called *homoousios*, 'of one substance' with God, but at best could be described as *homoiousios*, 'of like substance' with God. In the Nicene Creed of 325 CE the church rejected Arius' view of God. But his view of the world in its relationship to God is still powerfully present in our culture. In our day this idea of space and time led Rudolf Bultmann to propose a system of 'demythologising', stripping away the space/time language relating to God's activity and transposing it into a timeless idea of 'authentic existence'. The whole program of demythologising and the various ideologies which seek to speak of God in 'images', which people find comfortable in terms of gender, are similar attempts to deny the possibility of God's condescension to be with us and for us in space and time as the personal God of the incarnation.

Einstein contended with a similar problem in developing his theory of special relativity in confrontation with the prevailing Newtonian view of space/time. Einstein's theory shattered the receptacle notion of space/time, making it impossible to think of these categories as logical straight jackets which enclose the universe. His view of the world is directly opposite to that which sees it as enclosed from above by logically necessary notions of time and space. Instead of reality being described in terms of abstract propositions, Einstein understood it as a field of meaning consisting of relational continuities, rather than as patterns of static causality. What is 'scientifically' observable cannot be represented with scientific precision without reference to what lies outside observation altogether. In this context space/time/matter is able to absorb various patterns of order; without abrogating or contradicting each other they are meaningfully coordinated. This rejection by Einstein of the radical dualism inherent in Newtonian physics between space/time and matter has had a profound effect on the way in which we may speak of God in relationship to the world.

In the so called 'scientific' view, the world is understood as a closed system of mechanistic causality in which God's relationship to the world is portrayed as mythological (ie depicting the other-worldly in terms of this world), or in some anthropological category such as a subjective feeling. But in terms of Einstein's world view, events in this world are understood as occurring in a continuum of coordinated fields of meaning. Such a view of the world, contrary to the Newtonian view, does not by definition exclude interaction between God and the creature in terms of the space/time structure of human existence.

In the Christian tradition the incarnation is the place where God identifies with our humanity in the Son of God who at the same time does not cease to be God. In Christ God binds our this-worldly existence to God's own personal existence and recreates our human being in relationship to God's own being. God unites our human being in a personal union in Christ within space and time. In Christ our space/time structures are so organised in relation to God that we may think and speak with them of the transcendent ground of our existence.

Our human nature, understood in this context, is shown to have its ground in Christ through whom creation itself came into being (John 1:1-3). He is the basis of creation's rational order. His incarnation is the reconstitution of creation in its created relationship with God. Christ re-creates our human relationship with God at every stage of our human development, from conception to death and beyond death ('conceived by the Holy Ghost, born of the virgin Mary'). Such a theological context does not prescribe what ethical decisions Christians should make. But it does establish that human beings cannot be considered merely in terms of their biochemical make up. The situation of the embryo in the womb or the aged person cannot be described without reference to the ground of their being in Christ. It is the action of God in creation and reconciliation which both defines and sustains human beings in such a manner as to include a relationship with God at every stage of their existence.

Therefore 'is' and 'ought' statements cannot be separated, fact and value must be considered together as part of the integrated field of reality whose rationality is grounded in the Logos, the Word of God. What a person *is* is determined by the relationship with God which undergirds and sustains all life. To treat other human beings at whatever stage of life as a means and not as an end is to treat the relationship with God which constitutes the fundamental ground of their existence as a means and not as an end.

This view, of course, is contrary to the current 'scientific' ideology where the components of the ethical decision making process are deemed to consist of 'rational principles' accepted by reasonable people, and where matters of theological value are relegated from the public world of 'facts' to the privatised world of individual belief. This sharp distinction between facts and values is a hangover of the Enlightenment view of the world. The Enlightenment defined reality in terms of the presupposed autonomous human reason. In this context 'rights' are understood in terms of such notions as 'the public good' or 'the greatest happiness for the greatest number'. Law then comes to mean the will of the people as expressed by parliament and, by definition, is understood as the highest good.

The Christian church must reject such a facile view of 'rights' and the 'good'. The evidence of the effects of this ideology in the social disintegration of western society is apparent on every side. The situation will not be remedied by the church continuing tacitly to accept the alternatives presented by a self-serving media establishment or by the strident voices of the self-serving ideologues who pose as spokespersons for enlightened reason. The church must seek anew to articulate the truth of human life in its relationship to God at every stage of human development. This truth is grounded in the personal nature of God's action for and in behalf of humanity, in the acts of creation and reconciliation of the world in Christ. In the words of the *Basis of Union* (paragraph 3), it is so that the church may learn the depth and breadth of meaning in its 'acknowledgment' that

> The Uniting Church acknowledges that the faith and unity of the Holy Catholic and Apostolic Church are built upon the one Lord Jesus Christ. The Church preaches Christ the risen crucified One and confesses him as Lord to the glory of God the Father. In Jesus Christ God was reconciling the world to himself. In love for the world, God gave his Son to take away the world's sin . . .

Part Four

Reactions and Dialogue

Christh and the Cosmos: Law and Gospel

This paper was prepared in response to a request from the Lutheran Church of Australia/Uniting Church in Australia dialogue, June 1991. This request was for a paper on 'Christ and the Cosmos' in terms of paragraph 7 of Part 3 of the agreed statement on 'The Law and the Gospel'.[1]

The paragraph states,

> The view (ie the Reformed view) of the unity of gospel and law is directly related to the truth of the unity of God and of Christ. Law and gospel are one since both are the one will and act of God in his saving work towards man. Christ is mediator of the divine ordering of the universe from its beginning; he also as the eternal Son manifested in the flesh performed the reconciling mediation without cessation or diminution of his mediation of the divine ordering of the universe. Christ as mediator of creation and redemption is one and the same mediator. The incarnation was an extension of his empire (ie the creation). So the view of God and Christ as one, without conflicting or contradictory wills, leads to the view of the gospel and law as fundamentally one also.[2]

The emphasis in Calvin, which comes to expression in this paragraph of the agreed statement, reflects a differing approach to the questions raised by the relationship between law and gospel than that of Luther. These differences may also be said to characterise differences in the church from the earliest times between the Latin West and the Greek East. These differences

---

1. See the text of agreed statement in *Lutheran Theological Journal* 19/1, May, 1985: 34ff.
2. *Ibid*, 43.

can be illustrated in the conflict between Cyril of Alexandria and Nestorius and the differing attitudes as to what the dispute was about, evinced by participants in the debate from the East and the West respectively.

The 'becoming' of the Word in the flesh (John 1:14), in terms of the dispute between Cyril and Nestorius, revolved around the status of Mary being considered as the *Theotokos*. For Cyril this 'becoming' was fundamental to understanding the relationship between God and creation.

> He thus underwent birth with us and like us, and took unto himself the passing into being of his own flesh, not as needing a second beginning unto being (for the Word was in the beginning and was God) but, that he might gather together the human race, a second first fruits after the first one, born after the flesh of a woman.

> How, tell me, would He have been made flesh, except He had received birth from a woman, the laws of human nature calling Him thereto, and bodily existence being able no otherwise to have its beginning? . . . Our Law's nature sets us, yea rather, nature's Creator, for as of each of existing things is the kin to it born, so of ourselves too, and no otherwise (how could it be?). For nought of all what it willeth to accomplish is impracticable to the Divine and Ineffable Power, yet doth it proceed through what befits the nature of things that are, not dishonouring the laws set by itself.[3]

The soteriological interest in Cyril's position is obvious, but at the same time his interest is in defending the fact that the incarnation is a work of the holy Trinity. The incarnate one is

---

3. St Cyril, 'Five Tomes Against the Blasphemy of Nestorius', Tome 1, translated by members of the English Church, in *Library of the Fathers of the Holy Catholic Church* (Oxford: Parker & Rivingtons, 1881), 8.

the second person of the Trinity, the Son. If Nestorius was right and Mary was simply *Christotokos*, the mother of the flesh of Christ, then the flesh of Christ is not definitive of the person of the Son but can be predicated of any person of the Trinity, since Christ's human nature is co-joined with divine nature as such. Contrary to his intention of safeguarding God's deity Nestorius, in fact, as Cyril never tires of pointing out, divides the Godhead and deifies the creature. For if the unspecified nature of deity is incarnate in the Son, as distinct from the hypostasis of the Son, then God is divided by being circumscribed by time and space and humanity, in being co-joined with divinity, is deified. 'That which is co-worshipped is altogether other than that with which it is worshipped.'[4]

Cyril's synodical letters and the Tome of Pope Leo to Bishop Flavian were accepted by the Council of Chalcedon as definitive documents regarding Christian orthodoxy. As will be seen, this action ensured that the Nestorian question remained unresolved by the Council's action. For Pope Leo had a quite different view from that of Cyril in respect of Nestorius' errors. According to Leo Nestorius' problem was that he said the human nature of our Lord was joined to the divine nature only after birth. The Word assumed a human nature which had been born of the virgin, who thus could only be described as *Christotokos* not *Theotokos*. For Leo, the problem resided in the fact that there was a disjunction in terms of time between the orthodox view and the Nestorian view of the Son's birth. He does not question Nestorius' assumption that the christological question involves the problem of how the divine nature is united with the human nature. He accepts the problem as posed by Nestorius' answer.[5]

---

4. Cyril, *ibid*, Tome 2, 70.
5. Leo, Pope, Letters xxviii, commonly called 'The Tome', in *Library of Nicene and Post-Nicene Fathers*, vol XII. All quotes from Leo's sermons and letters follow this translation.

For Cyril the humanity of the Son defines the 'becoming' of the Son of God, since the soteriological purpose of the incarnation relates directly to the ontological renewal of humanity in relationship to the Father. On the other hand, for Leo the purpose of the incarnation is to establish a human nature that is innocent. It is the value of Christ's innocence in his undeserved death that is the focus of Leo's soteriology, dominated as it is by a distributive view of justice. The forensic framework of Leo's soteriology entails that the humanity of the Son of God plays a quite different role than in the thinking of Cyril. The latter's interest is in the ontological renewal of the creature in history through the work of the Spirit, celebrated in the church's liturgy.[6]

Luther's rediscovery of the doctrine of *simul justus et peccator* entails the whole of his theology being cast in a dialectic inherent in his understanding of the gospel. In a wealth of expressions which Luther employs we see how important this is to the coherence of his theological thought. *Regimen spirituale regimen corporale, regnum gratiae/regnum rationis, regnum fidei /regnum operum, regnum Christi regnum Caesaris, Hörreich/Sehreich* etc—the two regimes are not two magnitudes excluding each other or competing with each other for rule, but two over lapping aspects of the one *regnum dei invisible*. The kingdom of God assumes a dual aspect within the world, and each aspect is inseparable from the other whilst history lasts. Ultimately, eschatologically, there are not two kingdoms but one, God's kingdom. But it is of the utmost importance to distinguish the two kingdoms in this world of time and space, the world of fallen creation. To confuse the two kingdoms is a great mark of the anti-Christ. That may be brought about by the subordination of the spiritual kingdom to the worldly kingdom as amongst the Turks or, vice versa, with the pope. What the

---

6.   Leo, Letters xxxi, cxix; cxxiv. See also Sermon xxviii in W Bright, *Select Sermons of St Leo the Great on the Incarnation*, 2 ed (London: Masters & Co, 1886), 136f.

devil does in either case is to anticipate the last judgment of God by decisions made in this world, and this is the essence of sin. It is the refusal of faith and grace. It attempts a direct relationship with God in terms of this world.

The sharpness of the strife created by the gospel in its conflict with the world, inherent in the *justus et peccator* dialectic, meant that Luther had little sense of the new creation in Christ as an already accomplished fact. Luther's doctrine of *Anfechtung*, which corresponds with his view of faith, means that the believer has difficulty learning to live on the resurrection side of the cross.

The continuing controversy amongst Lutheran theologians as to the possibility of and the nature of a third use of the law apart from its negative functions, of restraining evil and convincing of sin, is a sign of an on-going question. Is the severe dialectic entailed in Luther's understanding of the Christian life as *simul justus et peccator* sufficient to present the rich texture of God's purposes in Christ for the renewal of creation? Is it possible to continue to maintain, as Henry Hamann indicated in his original paper on the subject of 'Law and Gospel', that the preaching of the gospel entails the 'separation of the kingdom on the left from the kingdom on the right, the keeping apart of the goodness of creation and the grace of redemption'?[7]

In teaching what later become known in the controversies between the Lutherans and the Reformed as the *extra Calvinisticum* (the Calvinist extra),[8] Calvin sought to emphasise several things. First that Christ is mediator of creation and redemption, second, that Christ is not known according to the way he is in himself, as one with the Father and the Spirit, but in the way in which he is for us, 'clothed with the gospel'.

---

7.   See 'Law and Gospel', *Lutheran Theological Journal* 19/1, 1985: 41. H Hamann's paper is unpublished. See also D Bonhoeffer, *Ethics* London: SCM, 1955), 79ff; 271ff.

8.   See E D Willis, *Calvin's Catholic Theology: the role of the so called extra Calvinisticum in Calvin's Theology* (Leiden: E J Brill, 1981).

If the gospel is the means which Christ uses to govern his chosen people, Christ as mediator of creation also rules the world beyond the church. But Calvin does not confuse the specific rule of Christ in the church by means of the gospel with a general ethic which would blur the distinction between the church and the world. Calvin believed sin had in fact weakened our will so that we do not have freedom to obey God's law naturally. The natural knowledge of the law leaves us without excuse. Apart from the gospel our consciences witness to the distance between our actions and God's will.

> Calvin does not hesitate to appeal to his readers to live according to the order of nature and the natural law, as well as according to the gospel. In making such an appeal to the natural he is not turning from Jesus Christ and the Scripture to some possible second and different source of guidance and inspiration.[9]

The basis of Calvin's claim for the relationship between creation and redemption, allowing for the continuities and discontinuities presupposed by God's act of reconciliation, is that God's relationship to the world is mediated in creation and redemption by the one Christ. He is not revealed to us in terms of his inner divine glory in which he shares the ineffable divine life with the Father and the Spirit, but as God in Christ clothed with the gospel. Therefore the relationship God establishes with the creature by the Word and Spirit does not relate to God's divine being and freedom as such, but to Christ and the Spirit. They 'accommodate' themselves in humility to the lowly estate of the creature in order to raise it to God's glory. This being the case, the created structures of human reason and experience

---

9.   R Wallace, *Calvin's Doctrine of the Christian Life* (Edinburgh: Oliver & Boyd, 1959), 144f.

become the means God uses to communicate God's self in acts of gracious union and communion.[10]

Hence Calvin's Christology and pneumatology arise from an acknowledgment of Christ's active and passive obedience whereby the whole work of his incarnation and the establishment of the church is the fulfilment of God's purpose for creation in relationship to himself. For example, in contrast to the prophets Christ received the Spirit without measure, not for his own sake in and for himself, for he is by nature ever one with the Spirit. He receives the Spirit for our sakes in order to sanctify in himself the flesh of our fallen human nature which he assumed from Mary. 'I sanctify myself that they may be sanctified in truth' (John 17:19).[11]

This voluntary self-emptying of the Son of God is the basis of the reconstituting act whereby the obedience of the second Adam replaces the wilful disobedience of the first Adam, in the humanity of Christ for our sake. Likewise Calvin believes that Christ's humanity was not relinquished by his ascension. For Christ did not need exaltation as the Son of God; he is ever one with the Father and the Spirit. He was and is exalted for our sake. He never ceased to be God and to rule the universe; he was exalted according to his manifestation for sinners as their High Priest.[12]

---

10. See T F Torrance, 'Knowledge of God and Speech about Him according to John Calvin', in *Theology in Reconstruction* (London: SCM, 1965).

11. J Calvin, *Institutes of the Christian Religion*, 2 vols (Grand Rapids: Eerdmans, reprint 1975), 2 13 2, and his comments on Hebrews chs. 3-5, Luke 1:15, and John 16:15, where Calvin distinguishes between Christ's 'hidden and intrinsic power' and 'that office which he has been appointed to exercise toward us'. Calvin, *Commentaries*, D W Torrance & T F Torrance eds, (Edinburgh: The St Andrew Press, 1963ff).

12. J Calvin, Institutes 2 13 2. Cf Commentary Hebrews 5:7. 'God the Father has appointed Christ "heir of all things" (Heb 1:2),

Calvin's use of the *extra Calvinisticum* ensured that he was able to give theological significance to the relative ethical judgments that Christians need to make without compromising the free grace of the gospel. The relationship between God and the creature established in Christ takes account of the relativities of the human situation. This situation has been and is presently mediated by the person of Jesus Christ who accommodates and continues to accommodate himself through the Holy Spirit to the created modes of human existence as the means whereby he wills to exercise his rule in the church and the world. The focus of theological coherence for Calvin is thus this-worldly and cosmic in its nature and scope.

On the other hand, Luther's understanding of the presence of Christ in the church and the world is surrounded by a strong dialectic in order to safeguard the freedom and Lordship, the grace of God, in relationship with the creature. This dialectic, expressed in various ways and in various spheres, entails that the relative moral decisions Christians make, the form of the Christian life within the created order, tend to be unrelated to the being of the Christian or the world in view of the cosmic import of Christ's redemption. Thus the law and the gospel tend to remain unrelated and separated. Consequently, the cosmic import of the gospel in Luther's theology is overshadowed by a strict dialectic which reinforces a forensic view of the cross. This eschews anything that confuses the law and the gospel and thereby seeks a 'theology of glory'.

---

according to his accommodation to our lowliness not according to His eternal divinity.'

A Comment on the *Interim Code of Ethics for Ministers*

There are three areas of concern that I wish to raise in respect of the *Interim Code of Ethics for Ministers*.[1] First, the *Code* and its supporting documentation offer no coherent account of an identifiable Christian basis for its ethical conclusions. Secondly, it is apparent that the *Code* is informed by a manner of ethical reasoning which shares the presuppositions about the human person that is common to post-Enlightenment thinking. Thirdly, the *Code* reinforces the view of the Christian faith as a privatised subjective option which has no relevance to the public questions of truth. It gives no indication upon what basis any claim to public truth of Christian ethical rests. I will address these areas of concern in the following.

James Gustafson in 1978 wrote an article titled *Theology Confronts Technology in the Life Sciences*.[2] In that article Gustafson observes that few people writing as 'ethicists' give explicit theological authorisation for their ethical perspectives. Most 'ethicists' write in such a manner that the relation of their moral discourse to any specific theological view is opaque. Gustafson notes that Christian ethicists try to justify the importance of theology in terms of the light it may cast on issues related to science and medicine. But Gustafson goes on to confess, 'I worked for years on a book, "Can Ethics be Christian?" with the nagging sense that most persons who answer in an unambiguous affirmative would not be interested in my supporting arguments. For those who believe the answer

---

1. *Interim Code of Ethics for Ministers of the Word, Deacons, Deaconesses, Youth Workers, Community Ministers and Lay Pastors in the Uniting Church in Australia.* Re-issued April 1998.
2. *Commonweal* 105/12, June 1978.

is negative the question itself is not sufficiently important to bother about'.

Reading the proposed *Interim Code of Ethics for Ministers* from the Assembly Commission on Women and Men, together with the 'Support Document for the Interim Code of Ethics 1997', one has the same nagging suspicion as infected Gustafson, as he pondered the question of the relationship between theology and ethics. The documentation from the Assembly is singularly bereft of any indication that what it is saying about 'ethics' is grounded in any recognisable understanding of the Christian community for whom pastoral relationships are grounded not in the church but in Christ. Christ is present with his people as their 'chief shepherd' in terms of his promises related to the preaching of the Word and the celebration of the two dominical sacraments. This paper is offered as an attempt to overcome this deficiency.

The meaning of the pastoral context derives directly from the fact that through baptism, the Eucharist and the preaching of the Word, Christ feeds and sustains his church on its journey towards its inheritance of fullness of life before his face. As the *Basis of Union* of the Uniting Church states in paragraph 6,

> The Uniting Church acknowledges that Christ has commanded his church to proclaim the gospel both in words and in the two visible acts of baptism and the Lord's Supper. He himself acts in and through everything that the Church does in obedience to his commandment.

Thus it may be said in paragraph 8 that 'the risen Lord feeds his baptised people on their way to the final inheritance of the kingdom'.

So the meaning of the words, 'pastoral context', is determined by the nature of the relationship established by the Good Shepherd, Jesus Christ, with his sheep, his people. The pastoral relationship is not established or maintained by us through the skills, gifts, and abilities we think or believe we may have been given in the various ministries of the church.

According to 1 Peter 2:25 Christ is the 'shepherd and guardian' of the church, as Jesus also describes himself in John 10. The manner in which the Shepherd guards and feeds the sheep is by his Word and Sacraments. John Calvin puts it this way:

> Jesus Christ is the only provision by which our souls are nourished. But because this is distributed by the Word of the Lord, which he has appointed as instrument to this end, it is also called bread and water. Now what is said of the Word fitly belongs also to the sacrament of the Supper, by means of which our Lord leads us to communion with Jesus Christ. For seeing we are so foolish, that we cannot receive him with true confidence of heart, when he is presented by simple teaching and preaching, the Father of his mercy, not at all disdaining to condescend in this matter to our infirmity, has desired to attach to his Word a visible sign, by which he represents the substance of his promises, to confirm and fortify us, and to deliver us from all uncertainty.[3]

It is in this way that we are to think of the pastoral context of the ministry. The pastoral context indicates the manner and the means by which the church is nourished and thus built up as the body of Christ. The Word of preaching and the sacraments are the means by which 'Christ constitutes and rules his church' (*Basis of Union*, Paragraph 4).

In the 'Introduction', Section 1, and in 'The Pastoral Relationship', Section 2, the *Interim Code of Ethics* emphasises the fact that ministers live and work within the church fellowship and are deeply involved in its interpersonal and administrative life. But it understands this, that is, the pastoral nature of the role of the minister, in psychological and sociological not theological terms.

---

3.   'Short treatise on the Holy Supper of our Lord and only Saviour Jesus Christ', in *Theological Treatises*, J K S Reid ed, (London: Westminster Press, 1954), 143ff.

The basic weakness of the document, as I see it, is that it fails to articulate the ecclesial context of its proposed code of ethics. Instead, it relies heavily on the corporate babel of modern management theory to describe the pastoral relationships in which the members of the Christian *koinonia* exist. As distinct from the promising beginnings in the 'Introduction', which attempts to locate the minister within the context of the life of the Christian community, the 'Support Document for the Interim Code of Ethics', which is meant to be read in conjunction with the Interim Code of Ethics, since it provides 'definitions for some of the terms used in the Interim Code, [and] limited comment on the content' (page 3), proceeds to describe the minister's behaviour within the context of the Christian community according to a 'code of ethics [which] stipulates the behaviour appropriate to a specific profession'. The code does not imply that ministers are particularly unethical; in its own words it seeks to be understood as a 'support [for] existing good practice'. The code then goes on to analyse the 'pastoral' relationship in which ministers find themselves resulting from the function they perform within the Christian community. This pastoral relationship is understood in terms of the idea of 'power'. Though the document says it does not intend to use the idea of 'power' in a pejorative sense. Yet it immediately sets out to describe the pastoral relationship in which ministers find themselves in terms of a 'power imbalance', due to such factors as their 'role', their 'gender', and their 'age', etc. These pastoral relationships, conceived in terms of 'power', are understood to be particularly sensitive to the implicit and explicit 'boundary' expectations of those involved. There then follows a series of case studies in which it is intended that those to whom the *Interim Code of Ethics* is directed should think about the way they act.

Stanley Hauerwas, a contemporary Christian writer on ethics, notes that contemporary ethical analysis concentrates on problems, situations in which it is hard to know what to do.[4] In such a context ethics is understood as a procedure for making decisions, for resolving conflict of choice situations. This model of ethics assumes that no one faces an ethical issue until they find themselves in a quandary: should I or should I not do this or that, adopt this stance or that. The moral life appears concerned primarily with hard decisions.

This picture of ethics is not accidental, according to Hauerwas, for the assumption that most of our moral concerns are 'problems' suggests that ethics can be construed as a rational science that evaluates alternative solutions. Moral decisions can then be seen to be resolvable on the basis of rationally derived principles that are not directly related to any particular set of moral convictions.

Ethics in this case can then be understood as a branch of decision theory, and can be taught as a disinterested social science. Hauerwas's criticism of current ethical theory aims at the influence of the Kantian ideal of rationally derived principles which are universally applicable. The problems associated with this standard account of moral reasoning, which in my judgement informs the methodology of the *Interim Code of Ethics*, are largely unnoticed because we have become conditioned by the tacit presuppositions of our culture that the individual rational self is that which endows the world with meaning.

Thus, from the perspective of the standard account, which is the object of Hauerwas's critique, such things as beliefs, dispositions and above all character cannot be the subject of rational analysis and are therefore seen as irrelevant to ethical discourse. They are subjective variants which need to be isolated from the process of ethical decision making. It seems that one only needs to state the implications of the standard

---

4. *A Community of Character: Toward a Constructive Christian Social Ethic* (Notre Dame Ind: University of Notre Dame), 1981.

account of ethical reasoning to see that it is inadequate from the perspective of Christian ethics.

We cannot account for moral decision making solely in terms of the rationality of the decision making process. We need to take into account those factors which form us as the people we are. It is these tacit factors, which make up who we are, which will determine what kind of moral considerations we will regard as rational and consequently to which we will give weight in our moral decision making.

For example, the language that we use to describe our behaviour to others and ourselves is not uniquely ours. We share a common cultural and social context which makes it possible for us to communicate with each other. So what makes it possible for us to check the truthfulness of others and our account of their moral behaviour is the personal relationships and the social context in which our moral ideas gain their credibility. We cannot, in other words, make our behaviour mean anything we want. Even what we may think is the most reasonable action must make sense not only to us, but must be congruent with the assumptions and beliefs embedded in the language which we use.

Another example is this paper. This paper is not written for Mr & Ms Everyone, but rather for those who find themselves in one way or another part of the Christian community, called the church. Thus it is not simply a matter of addressing an audience who hears what I am saying, but rather the claim for truthfulness of Christian ethics requires for its intelligibility the practices of the Christian community. This context is vital for understanding Christian ethics. Christian ethics only makes sense in the context of those who have learned that their salvation comes through the worship of Jesus Christ. Thus Christian ethics is first of all not concerned with justice, though Christians obviously seek justice, but rather their primary concern is to be faithful disciples of Jesus Christ. This may entail that Christian ethics, instead of making Christians functional within the morès of liberal democracies, will make them dysfunctional!

In both of these examples the point is that it is impossible to make sense of ethical discourse on the basis of the standard account which sees it as a variety of decision theory applied to situations in which it is difficult to choose. The standard account assumes that such things as beliefs, dispositions, and above all character, cannot be the subject of rational analysis and are therefore seen as irrelevant to ethical discourse. They are subjective variants which need to be isolated from the process of ethical decision making.[5]

Now what Hauerwas and, in his own way, Yoder are saying in their critique of the standard account of ethical reasoning is not some slick marketing trick. In order to indicate this I want to look at the New Testament understanding of the context of Christian existence in terms of the *koinonia* or community of the church.

In the New Testament the church is seen as a historical reality created by God's action in the incarnation, life, death and resurrection of Jesus Christ and the gift of the Holy Spirit. The church is understood as a people of the New Covenant created by these events. It is a sign in the old creation that a new future for creation has been opened up by the resurrection of Jesus Christ. Those who are members of the *koinonia* already experience this coming new creation in a form of life which distinguishes itself by the nature of the relationships between the members.

1 John 3:14 says that 'we know that we have passed from death to life because we love one another'.[6] This understanding of the basis of the church's life transforms the familiar metaphor of 'the Body' from simply one which

---

5.   Cf J H Yoder, *The Politics of Jesus*, 2nd edition (Grand Rapids: Eerdmans, 1998).

6.   All biblical quotes are from the *Revised Standard Version of the Bible* unless otherwise indicated (Nashville: Nelson, 1989).

points towards the church's essential unity to one which also indicates a new fellowship between Jesus Christ and believers (1 Cor 12:26-27; 1 Peter 2:4-10). There is no real presence of Jesus in history apart from those who are joined to him in His Body. The church as this reality does not yet appear in history as what it shall be. 'For here we have no continuing city, but we seek the city which is to come' (Hebrews 13:14). Nevertheless, the New Testament has no doubt that the coming reign or rule of Christ is present and active in this age in and for the church and the world. In Ephesians we read:

> This is the reason that I, Paul, am a prisoner for Christ Jesus for the sake of you Gentiles—for surely you have already heard of the commission of God's grace that was given me for you, and how the mystery was made known to me by revelation, as I wrote above in a few words, a reading of which will enable you to perceive my understanding of the mystery of Christ. In former generations this mystery was not made known to humankind, as it has now been revealed to his holy apostles and prophets by the Spirit: that is, the Gentiles have become fellow heirs, members of the same body, and sharers in the promise in Christ Jesus through the gospel (vv 1-6).
>
> Of this gospel I have become a servant according to the gift of God's grace that was given me by the working of his power. Although I am the very least of all the saints, this grace was given to me to bring to the Gentiles the news of the boundless riches of Christ, and to make everyone see what is the plan of the mystery hidden for ages in God who created all things; so that through the church the wisdom of God in its rich variety might now be made known to the rulers and authorities in the heavenly places. This was in accordance with the eternal purpose that he has carried out in Christ Jesus our Lord, in whom we

have access to God in boldness and confidence through faith in him . . . (vv 7-12).

I therefore, the prisoner in the Lord, beg you to lead a life worthy of the calling to which you have been called, with all humility and gentleness, with patience, bearing with one another in love, making every effort to maintain the unity of the Spirit in the bond of peace. There is one body and one Spirit, just as you were called to the one hope of your calling, one Lord, one faith, one baptism, one God and Father of all, who is above all and through all and in all. But each of us was given grace according to the measure of Christ's gift . . . for building up the body of Christ, until all of us come to the unity of the faith and of the knowledge of the Son of God, to maturity, to the measure of the full stature of Christ. We must no longer be children, tossed to and fro and blown about by every wind of doctrine, by people's trickery, by their craftiness in deceitful scheming. But speaking the truth in love, we must grow up in every way into him who is the head, into Christ, from whom the whole body, joined and knit together by every ligament with which it is equipped, as each part is working properly, promotes the body's growth in building itself up in love (4:1-7, 12-16).

In this passage from Ephesians we see how the writer understands the character of the *koinonia* of the church to be derived from the church understood as the Body of Christ. The *koinonia* of the church is the fellowship creating reality of Christ's presence in the world. According to the writer this *koinonia* has a cosmic significance as God's secret plan for the universe. This plan, hidden to past generations, is now made plain in the fact that Jews and Gentiles are fellow heirs of God's covenanted promises. The existence of such a *koinonia* is a sign for the whole creation of its promised renewal through the fulfilment of God's reconciling purpose in Christ.

The goal of *koinonia* as the church lives its life in history is, according to the passage, 'maturity'. This maturity is the fruit of the church's unity with the faith and knowledge of the Son of God; maturity is the manner in which the life of Christ himself, his faith and knowledge, configures and forms the members of his Body. Maturity is measured by the development towards what is called the 'fullness of Christ', or as the NRSV puts it, 'the full stature of Christ'.[7] This entails that the *koinonia* confirms its cosmic purpose, as the scope of its existence, by 'building itself up in love'. This occurs as Christ the Head of the Body does his work within it. This is the ethical implication of the life of the church, understood as the Body of Christ, according to this passage from Ephesians.

We come at this point to a conclusion which has far reaching implications for our understanding of Christian ethics. It is this, that *Christian ethics aims not at morality but maturity in the Christian life.* Thus the pastoral relationship cannot by definition be understood in terms of an 'imbalance of power' as indicated in the *Code of Ethics.* The power that is effective in the relationships within the church is the power of Christ who did not please himself, but gave himself up for us all. Or, as St Paul puts it in Galatians 6:2, 'Bear one another's burdens, and so fulfil the law of Christ'; and in Romans 15:3, 'For Christ did not please himself; but, as it is written, "The reproaches of those who reproached thee fell on me"'. Or the writer of the Epistle to the Ephesians describes the mystery of faith in this way:

> But speaking the truth in love, we must grow up in
> every way into him who is the head, into Christ, from
> whom the whole body, joined and knit together by
> every ligament with which it is equipped, as each part
> is working properly, promotes the body's growth in
> building itself up in love (4:15,16).

The contrast in the text is between the maturity of bodily growth in an adult and the incomplete development of a child.

---

7.   *New Revised Standard Version.*

The writer appropriates the organic relationship between the two states in order to illuminate the organic nature of the relationships of the *koinonia*. We may thus summarise the thought of the writer in this way: Christian maturity is the integrity of relationships within the *koinonia* which allows each member to be who they are in relationship to the other. On this basis the writer goes on in 4:25-31 and chapter 5, to indicate, across a wide cross section of human inter-relatedness, the practical implications of this truth.

Such a contextual approach to understanding human beings as primarily inter-related makes for a radical shift of perspective in ethical thought. It is an approach which first of all looks at who human beings *are* in their relationship to God in Jesus Christ, and consequently who they are in relationship to each other. This approach is based on the *indicative*, the great 'therefores' of St Paul's logic in Romans. There, immediately after describing the new being of the Christian in relationship to Christ, he begins his exhortations on the assumption that those to whom he is speaking have been claimed by and live in Christ through their union with him in baptism.

> For we know that Christ, being raised from the dead, will never die again; death no longer has dominion over him. The death he died he died to sin, once for all, but the life he lives he lives to God. So you also must consider yourselves dead to sin and alive to God in Christ Jesus. Let not sin therefore reign in your mortal bodies, to make you obey their passions. (Romans 6:9).

Paul's logic is, 'because you are mine, therefore', in contrast to the simple *imperative*, 'do this or that because it is commanded', or 'do this or that and you will be worthy to be called Christian'. No, Paul's logic is: because Christ has claimed you in baptism, because you are his, therefore live in this way and not that. This does not imply that in this approach there are no ethical demands or norms. The church still lives its life as the unredeemed in an unredeemed world; the church is made up of justified sinners. But it does mean that such ethical demands which shape the life of the Christian *koinonia* acquire their authority from the specific personal relationships constituted by the action of Christ and the Spirit.

By grounding the integrity of Christian ethics in the relationships constitutive of the *koinonia*, understood as the Body of Christ, the church is not cut off from the world. *The ecclesial context of Christian ethics does not imply that the claims of Christian ethics relate to the church as a ghetto, whilst the world is left to its own devices.*

The relationship between the church and the world that I wish to explore at this point is one which seeks to understand how the church and the world are related in terms of who Jesus Christ is both as the Creator Word and the Reconciler of the world to God. In Genesis 1-11 the basic form of human being is understood to be one of relatedness—to God and to other human beings, to animals and to the earth. This is a fundamental characteristic of what it is to be human. This relatedness is grounded in the fact that human beings come from God, who in terms of God's own life is a God who is not simply one—a Monad—but is fundamentally a relational God. God as revealed in Jesus Christ is a God who from all eternity has chosen not to be God alone but to be God in relationship: to be God as both One and Another in the unity of a Third, a blessed Trinity. This relatedness of God; God's being for the Other is the ground of the creatures' relatedness and makes possible the creatures' being human in these terms in relationship to God and in relationship to each other as man and woman (cf the *imago Dei* of Genesis 1:26-27).

Now the relationship between the context of Christian ethics considered as the ethics of the *koinonia* of the Body of Christ and the world is grounded in Christ's and the Spirit's relationship to the world as its Creator and Sanctifier. The church lives its life within the world as one among a host of other institutions and options which provide contexts for human relatedness, but the relationship of the church and the world is alone to be understood as providing the world with its purpose and meaning. John Calvin puts it this way,

> Christ was endued with the Holy Spirit in a unique manner, in order to separate us from the world, and introduce us into the hope of an eternal inheritance. Hence, the Spirit is called the Spirit of holiness, not only because He animates us and supports us by that general power which is displayed in mankind, and in all other creatures, but because He is the seed and root of the heavenly life within us.[8]

Calvin here indicates that the relationship between the church considered as the Body of Christ and the world is grounded in the work of the Spirit in creation and reconciliation. But the Spirit as the sanctifier of Christians is dependent on the action of sanctification of our humanity in the obedience of the Son of God in his earthly journey from Bethlehem to Golgotha, receiving the Spirit and sanctifying our flesh at every stage of our human development. It is the continuity and discontinuity between creation and redemption defined by the unique work of the Son of God that establishes and maintains the essential structure of the relationship between the church and the world. According to Calvin Christ is the Mediator of creation before He is clothed with our humanity.

> Thus we understand that the name Mediator applies to Christ not only because He took our flesh or because He undertook the office of reconciling the human race to God. But already from the beginning of creation he was truly Mediator . . . because He held primacy even over angels and was the first born of creatures. Eph 1:2; Col 1:15; Col 2:10. Whence we conclude that He began to perform the office of Mediator not only after the fall of Adam, but in so far as He is the eternal Son of God, angels as well as men

---

8. *Institutes of the Christian Religion* (Grand Rapids: Eerdmans, 1975), Book 3 1 2.

are united to God by Him in order that they may remain upright.[9]

Here we see Calvin's insistence that in the incarnation the Son of God left heaven in such a manner that he continued to exercise his office as the *Mediator of Creation.* The incarnation is thus an extension of Christ's domain, not his temporary abdication from it. It is in this that we must see the primary theological key to understanding the relationship between the ecclesial context of Christian ethics and their relationship to the world. We must see that the church's primary purpose is to indicate by its being and action, its practice of Christian maturity, that creation's vocation is to be found in its becoming the Body of Christ. The tremendous claim made in the New Testament is that the existence of the church is the secret of the existence of all things, the church's vocation is cosmic in scope. That is the church, consisting of Jews and Gentiles as the inheritors of the promises made by God to Israel.

> . . . and to make all see what is the plan of the mystery hidden for ages in God who created all things; that through the church the manifold wisdom of God might now be made known to the principalities and powers in the heavenly places. This was according to the eternal purpose which he has realised in Christ Jesus our Lord (Eph 3:9-11).

In his book, *The Nature of Doctrine,*[10] George Lindbeck writes that Christianity must 'absorb' the world. What he means is that a Christian understanding of reality must be the place from which all reality is understood. If Christianity is to be self-consistent it must take Jesus Christ as the human expression of God's reality and truth. This seeming imperialist claim on the part of Christianity is simply a way of giving expression to the fact that in any particular culture what is most real, what is

---

9.   'Reply to the Polish Brethren', *Calvin: opera quae supersunt omnia,* G Baum et al eds, (Berlin, 1863-1900), 9 338.

10.   Philadelphia: Westminster Press, 1984.

important will be defined by the dominant world view. It may not be the view of the majority of the inhabitants of any given society but it will be the view which gives meaning to the public culture and the issues of the public agenda which are seen to be important. It will articulate a worldview that absorbs the world.

The world which we inhabit, that is the culture of the society in which we live, is one which is pervasively influenced by the 'modern' world view, that is a view of reality which derives from the Enlightenment. Reality is that which can be defined by our measurement of it. The material world can be described accurately by us in terms of models which are basically mechanical and mathematical. The reality of the other person is less real than our own mind and thought. From this disembodied position everything else whether persons or things are useable and or discardable. As Colin Gunton points out,[11] 'modernity is characterised by a philosophy of non-relation, of disengagement, in which human subjects standing apart from each other and the world use each other and the world as instruments'.

The modern penchant for the economic philosophy called 'monetarism' or economic rationalism, as the panacea of all social and economic questions, is the old idea of Adam Smith's 'hidden hand' of market forces in modern dress. It assumes that we do not belong to God and each other but are our own; this entails that others are there for whatever purposes happen to be marketable.

The dominant view of our culture is that we are the world: we absorb the world and give it meaning at the expense of community and the natural environment. Postmodernism in its critique of modernity came to prominence as a consequence of its recognition that the world as it is in itself, the world apart from our description of it, is inaccessible to human beings. Thus

---

11. *The One, The Three and the Many* (Cambridge University Press, 1993), 12.

the schools of postmodernity view language as to all intents and purposes the only reality. The attempt is made to shift attention from study of the world as an objective entity to the study of texts and the various cultural linguistic realities which make up the world. The world is not *the* world but a multitude of small textual worlds; the linguistic worlds in which we live and move and have our being. Thus there is no such thing as the truth. There is merely this truth or that truth according to the operating context; there is my truth and your truth. All we have recourse to is a shifting sea of relativities none of whose views can be compared critically.

The problem with such views as purveyed by some post modern critics of modernity is that just such claims as they make presuppose the very God's eye view of which they are so critical and which they intend their account of language to refute. It is a classic example of the famous Cretan saying, 'all Cretans are liars'.

Despite their seemingly opposite views of reality, the modern and postmodern world views share the notion that human reason can be the final arbiter of what is real or true. In place of the Enlightenment or modern view that 'what I see is what is there', that reason is a window onto a universal state of affairs, the postmodern view is that 'my facts' are 'my facts' and 'your facts' are 'your facts'. The world of postmodernism consists of many worlds, many contexts, and many truths.

Whilst postmodernism offers valuable criticism of the dogmatism of reason based on the Enlightenment view of the world it, too, is subject to the same danger of the dogmatism of reason. Relativism and its colleague, political correctness, now replace the old fashion idea of factual correctness. The problem with the culture of postmodernity is that, whereas modern culture assumed that there could be dispute about 'the facts' of the case and a sense of the commonality of the language used to describe the facts, now whole groups of people regard themselves as immune from criticism. At the same time they treat other groups of people as tools or objects to be stereotyped, or in other ways minimised or ridiculed. To some feminists all men are rapists and men are not allowed to object to this label; some ethnic groups label all members of what is perceived as the dominant racial group as oppressors and exploiters who cannot do or say anything to exonerate themselves. Prejudice, intolerance, and abuse may not be new phenomena associated with human relationships but post modernism insulates such behaviour from any criticism. As Gunton has astutely observed, some of the more strident examples of post modern criticism amount to no more than a corporate or group veneer on the presuppositions of modernity.[12]

Now, in the context of a culture in which the predominant views are alien to the presuppositions of Christian claims, it is important to see that human life has a characteristic unity and purpose which establishes who people are as persons in relationship to God and each other. This unity is not a creation of the human mind, or an arbitrary choice of some group interest, but derives from the nature of Christ and the Spirit as God's personal presence with and for the creature in creation and reconciliation and promised redemption. By this personal presence of Christ and the Spirit there is established in history a context in which a narrative or story of human personhood becomes the truth of human relationships to God and each other. This context and this reality is the Body of Christ, the sacred mystery of the church. The answer to the question, 'What am I to do'? is 'I am to do what I am become'. We are to act in accordance with what it has been *given to us to be* as members of the Body of Christ.

Christian ethics therefore raises claims of public truth. It is not to be trivialised as an expression of 'professional good practice' for the privileged fellowship of the church. The claims of Christian ethics cannot be separated from the cosmic purpose of creation as both the fulfilled and also the yet to be realised

---

12.   *Op cit.*

reconciliation and redemption of the church in Christ. Unless this is understood to be the function of ethical discourse within the Christian community its claims becomes irrelevant to the world in which its mission is set.

> But you are a chosen race, a royal priesthood, a holy nation, God's own people, that you may declare the wonderful deeds of him who called you out of darkness into his marvellous light. Once you were no people but now you are God's people; once you had not received mercy but now you have received mercy. Beloved, I beseech you as aliens and exiles to abstain from the passions of the flesh that wage war against your soul. Maintain good conduct among the Gentiles, so that in case they speak against you as wrongdoers, they may see your good deeds and glorify God on the day of visitation. Be subject for the Lord's sake to every human institution, whether it be to the emperor as supreme, or to governors as sent by him to punish those who do wrong and to praise those who do right. For it is God's will that by doing right you should put to silence the ignorance of foolish people. Live as free people, yet without using your freedom as a pretext for evil; but live as servants of God (1 Peter 2:9-16).

New Age?

What is New Ageism?[1] To some people the term conjures up in their minds images of healing crystals, reincarnation, Shirley MacLaine, Maharishi and his entourage, astrology, rebirthing, or any other of a number of things from the bizarre to the downright loopy. New Ageism is, in fact, as diverse as the Christian church itself. It may be that to even speak of New Ageism at all, given the wide variety of sects, movements and individuals to which it is taken to refer, involves using somewhat of a misnomer.

Yet the phenomenon remains, whatever we wish to call it and however we categorise it. The influence of the movement is felt in the church, in health care, in education, in the environmental movement, in business and in personal management. Marilyn Ferguson whose book *The Aquarian Conspiracy* is widely regarded as a textbook of New Ageism,[2] and the writings of the former Dominican priest Mathew Fox,[3] are representative of the movement or, as Ferguson calls it, the 'conspiracy', even though in some respects there would be a quite serious divergence in their views.

Borrowing the expression 'paradigm shift' from the physical sciences it may be said that New Agers seek new frameworks for understanding and explaining particular aspects of reality and human experience. For example, there is a common tendency to relate New Age thought, and its relationship to the

---

1. I am indebted to the comments of my colleague at Trinity College, Brisbane, Rev Dr D I Rankin, for what follows.
2. See E Peters, 'Discerning the Spirits of the New Age', *The Christian Century*, Aug-Sept 1988: 2.
3. M Fox, *Original Blessing* (Santa Fe: Bear & Co, 1983); *The Coming of the Cosmic Christ* (Melbourne: Collins Dove, 1989); *A Spirituality Named Compassion and the Healing of the Global Village, Humpty Dumpty and Us* (Minneapolis: Winston Press, 1979).

way in which Western and particularly Protestant Christian thought has developed, to the relationship between Newtonian views of absolute space and time and the mechanistic, rationalistic view of human life and thought based on this framework which has been replaced by the Einsteinian relational universe where everything is connected (the Nexus) and governed by a 'wise uncertainty'.[4]

New Ageism speaks of an underlying web of connectedness in the universe which represents the true reality: the need to connect with the source of life and the importance of mystical experience to provide a direct connection, an unmediated access, to the source or centre or ground of being itself. Consequently, there is an emphasis on 'centring' exercises, relaxation and fantasy; discovering a way home whereby the alienated self addresses the wholeness it has lost. So, for example, authentic education in the church is not about imparting knowledge but about 'educing' or drawing forth that which is already known in the hidden depths of being. For Mathew Fox Jesus is historically unique because he broke through completely into his God consciousness, into an awareness of his own innate divinity, which quality he shares with all humanity. For Fox the cosmic Christ is not the person of the Son of God incarnate in the flesh of Jesus. The cosmic Christ 'is the divine pattern that connects in the person of Jesus Christ (but by no means is limited to that person)'.[5] For Fox the historic person of Jesus is no more than the supreme example of divine consciousness. The historical Jesus merely shows us how to birth the presence of the cosmic Christ.

Underlying this understanding of the world and the place of Jesus Christ is what may be called a monistic cosmology. Fundamental for the Christian view of the world is the distinction between God and the world, that is, the world is

---

4.   M Ferguson, *The Aquarian Conspiracy* (Los Angeles: J P Tarcher, 1987), 327.

5.   Fox, *The Coming of the Cosmic Christ, op cit*, 135.

created, contingent, creaturely and dependent upon a free act of God's will for its original and continued existence. Mathew Fox speaks of the world in terms which he describes as *panentheistic*. 'God is in everything and everything is in God'.[6] He pictures this idea as a circle of water with fish in it. We are the fish, God is the water. Like the water passing through the gills of a fish, we breathe God in and out all day long. The world is thus a mode in which God comes to expression.[7] Panentheism sees all events and beings as divine. To avoid being accused of pantheism, of a view where the world is identified with God, Fox uses the word *transparence* to include what he means by God's difference from and his immanence in the world.

Some Responses to New Age Claims About the Nature of the World and the Place of Human Beings in it

The following remarks are intended to raise what are understood to be important questions that need to be addressed to New Age thought.

- The nature of the creation and the relationship of God to the creation as understood in the Bible and Christian tradition.
- The place of Jesus Christ in the relationship between God and creation.
- The nature of the human condition in the Christian tradition.

1. Perhaps the most attractive feature of New Age teaching is its emphasis on wholeness, both in personal and global terms. The development of European thought since the Enlightenment has emphasised the priority of reason and rationality in a manner which divides and fragments consciousness of the world's inter-relatedness, blurring the connections between objective and subjective, body and mind, individual and community, humanity and nature. But interwoven with this there are serious deficiencies in New Age thought about the

---

6. Fox, *Original Blessing, op cit,* 90.
7. Fox, 'Panentheistic Spirituality: Religious Education for the Future', *Living Light,* Fall ed, 1974: 357-67.

world and its relationship to God from an orthodox Christian perspective.

There is good reason why Christians have distanced themselves from the view that the world and God are so inter-related that the world, as in Mathew Fox's thinking, becomes a manifestation of divinity and the focus of the creature's relationship with God in the possession of a common divinity, albeit in a differing form. Such a view negates the fact that the world is created by God out of nothing (*ex nihilo*), as the early church taught. Why is this so?

Fundamentally, the biblical view of God as the Creator of the world, and therefore of the world as not divine or a part of divinity, is that *the God of the Bible is a gracious God*. That is to say, God's relationship to the world is one based in God's freedom. God did not need the world in order to be God; God is not dependent upon the world in order to be God. The world exists because God willed to love the world. That the world is created and not an extension of God's divinity means that God's love for the world is free; it is not motivated in any way apart from the fact that God willed to love the world.

If the world was an extension of God's divinity it would be the case that in relating to the world God would be relating to God's self. God's love would then be a form of self-love and God would then need the world in order to be fully God. In that case, God could not be gracious to the world, for in acting towards the world God would be loving God's self. But the biblical tradition of the Old and New Testaments is that God has acted and acts graciously towards the world and its people. God's gracious action in calling Israel and becoming incarnate in the person of God's Son, Jesus Christ, was to fulfil God's relationship with Israel as a relationship for all people. Here we find the basis of the church's view that the world is created and not semi-divine.

2. The place of Jesus Christ in the relationship between God and the world is decisive for Christian faith. It is decisive because the church believes that in the person of God's Son

God, in an act of inestimable freedom, stooped to accommodate God's being to the totality of the human condition in all its estrangement from God. This action of God is not to be understood as deriving from some inner need of God for a relationship with the world. This action indicates that the creature's relationship with God is far from being one in which the creature has, in its own being, access to some divine ground of being by mystical manipulation or meditative exercise. It is a relationship which is wholly dependent from beginning to end on God's gracious condescension. If this is not the case then the incarnation of Jesus Christ, the shedding of God's blood on the cross and his resurrection from the dead are completely unnecessary. New Age theologians claim that Jesus is simply the paradigm of the truth we all share with him, in as much as he simply shows us how to kick-start our natural relationship with the divinity which is in us all. If this is so it would appear that the existence of Jesus Christ as the mediator of the creature's relationship with God is unnecessary. This is not in keeping with the church's tradition concerning the place of Jesus Christ in the relationship of human beings with God and with each other.

3. In the light of God's action in Jesus Christ the Christian tradition does not see the world as essentially whole; something which New Age thinkers presuppose as the basis of their view of the world. The action of God in Christ indicates that the relationship of the world to God is one of brokenness, alienation, and estrangement. God gets crucified in the world! God's Son is given up for the sake of the world in an act of inestimably costly love. This brokenness is not an illusion that can be corrected through exercises in consciousness-raising and self-realisation. The power to heal the human situation in the world does not lie in the situation but in the gracious gift of God's self in God's Son.

Our harassed contemporaries, do not find in whatever depths they plumb the divinity so easily claimed by New Age thinkers and theologians. What is found? Loneliness and lostness, the horrifying indifference of nature. Of love at the ground of being there is found not a trace. The frightfulness of nature and history are brought home in graphic detail to our contemporaries by every TV news segment. Neither by looking around nor by looking deep do they find any reason at all to trust in the ground of their being. That, however, in the age of Auschwitz and Hiroshima, Idi Amin, Pol Pot, Vietnam, the Gulag Archipelago, Waco, and East Timor is their real question. The most serious problem for many of our contemporaries is that experience of the world and contemplation of the depths do not give any confirmation that love is the ground of being. Nor do they confirm that they—these poor lonely mortals, oppressed by nature, impulses and powers of all kinds—are loved from all eternity. New Agers treat this central declaration of the Christian faith as something easily accessible, whereas it is surely the most unselfevident, most extraordinary thing of all. In fact, it can be believed only in the teeth of reality as it is experienced by human beings. There must be extraordinary authorisation for such a thing to be seriously maintained and lived by. It is an authorisation which does not spring from us speaking about ourselves in a rather loud voice, but from the gracious gift of God who faithfully maintains commitment to the creation both in preserving and finally reconciling it through Jesus Christ, in whom alone it finds its fulfilment.

Person and the Trinity: Comments on J Zizioulas, 'On Being a Person: Towards an Ontology of Personhood'[1]

John Zizioulas begins to delineate the parameters of his discussion of the theological significance of personal being by a critical examination of its significance for Greek thought. This discussion is important since it relates directly to the cultural factors with which Christians in the Western world must contend in the formulation and articulation of the gospel.

This discussion takes up the question of personal being, its status and meaning in terms of the philosophical presuppositions of Greek (and Western) thought. The discussion derives its relevance from the fact that Western culture is largely dominated by the rise in Europe of democratic nation states consequent on the break up of medieval Europe as a result of the Reformation and subsequent religious wars, the rise of Rationalism and Romanticism in theology and philosophy, and the French Revolution of the eighteenth century. Democracy appeared as the political option which enabled people both to be protected by social contract and to achieve ordinary human goals. Democracy presented itself as decent mediocrity over against authoritarian monarchs and absolute states with splendid corruption and unrelieved oppression.

The personal identity of an individual in democratic theory is not established by that theory; all citizens are assumed to be autonomous, creating values for themselves by the exercise of reason. For example, the American Declaration of

---

1.   Essay of the same title in *Persons, Divine and Human: Kings Essays in Theological Anthropology* C Schwoebel ed, (Edinburgh: T&T Clark, 1991), 33ff.

219

Independence holds self evident truths to be the basis of its rationality: 'We hold these truths to be self-evident, that all men are created equal, that they are endowed by their Creator with certain unalienable Rights, that among these are Life, Liberty, and the pursuit of Happiness'.

The individual in a democratic society becomes the agent for creating value. The individual creates meaning by adopting a lifestyle of which there is not one but many possible variants. The individual who has a lifestyle can command esteem, the individual's own and that of others. Woody Allen's comedy is a set of variations on the theme of the person who does not have a real self or identity and feels superior to the unauthentic 'adjusted' people who surround him. He regards himself as superior because he is self-conscious of his situation, in not having an identity, yet at the same time feels inferior to others because they seem comfortable in their adjustment to society. Woody Allen's haunted comedy diagnoses the dilemmas of human beings in a democracy; they stem from the autonomous self who, in order to create meaning, must posit its own identity by creating values or lifestyles. Its great strength is in depicting the self-conscious role player, never quite at home in a role—interesting because there is this constant quest to be like others, who are yet ridiculous because they are unaware of their emptiness.

The question one poses for Woody Allen is whether his humour only helps us to feel comfortable with the nihilism he so astutely observes at the heart of liberal democratic values.[2] Words such as 'lifestyle', 'identity', and 'commitment' are now practically everyday words used by people seeking to articulate their understanding of life. The most popular schools of psychology and their therapies take value-positing as the standard of healthy personality—not realising that it is

---

2. On this question see the penetrating analysis in A MacIntyre, *After Virtue: A study in Moral Theory* (Notre Dame Ind: University of Notre Dame Press, 1981).

precisely this question which belies the emptiness which the therapy seeks to heal. The crisis in people's identity in mass culture cannot be overcome by pretending that the void is simply the absence of positive self-affirmation. Such answers in terms of 'lifestyle', 'commitment' etc, must assume a value which is not relative in order to overcome the nothingness caused by the relativity and emptiness of the democratic experience. But since the social sciences are built upon the premise of value relativism, there can be no rational basis for asserting any value which is of permanent validity. There is no doubt that this malaise, which leads to scientific and philosophical indifference to good and evil, also afflicts the church's self-understanding. God becomes intellectually irrelevant or is relevant only in terms of privatised religious lifestyle options.[3]

Zizioulas' contention is that the philosophical background to the debates about the trinitarian dogma in the early church have relevance to the issues of contemporary interest since they bear on the same issues of personal identity. The dogma of the Trinity was worked out by the church in a cultural context which had many similarities with the questions of personal identity found in modern democratic culture. In Platonic thought, the idea of personal being is impossible since the soul which ensures one's identity is not permanently united with the individual. The soul lives eternally and can be united with other concrete individuals by reincarnation. With Aristotle the idea of person is impossible precisely because the soul is united with the individual. The individual endures so long as the psychosomatic union endures. Death dissolves the union definitively. The person has no enduring reality. The reason for the inability of Greek thought to endow human individuality with permanence lay in the view that being constitutes a unity in spite of the multiplicity of appearances. Greek thought is monistic. God and the world are bound together in the unity of

---

3.   *Ibid*, 6ff.

being. In such a view human freedom is an impossible predicate of existence, yet it is a necessary precondition of being a person.

This contradiction in Greek culture is the recurrent theme of the Greek tragedies. It is here that the word 'person' appears. Person (*prosopon*) is identified as the actor's mask. The theatre is the setting for the conflict between human freedom and the rational unity of thought and being. The question addressed in the tragedies is: 'how can the human strive to be free, to rise above the rational unity, the necessity grounded in the unitary nature of all being?' The battle is engaged between human beings, nature, and the gods. It is here that human beings learn there is no escape from their fate. The human being cannot continue to show *hubris* (individuality, pride) in the presence of the gods. Human freedom is illusory, consequently the *prosopon* is nothing but a mask.

Similarly Roman thought, influenced as it is by Greek thought, sees the *persona* of the individual as the role played in the social and legal relationships which constitute the corporate state. The Roman idea of *persona* expresses the problem of necessity and freedom involved in understanding the idea of the human person by maintaining that to submit to the organised whole is to ensure oneself of the possibility of personhood. This analysis is not far removed from the contemporary culture of which we have already spoken. For example, the sociology of our time cannot be understood without reference to this Roman idea of *persona*. Sociology understands society as a series of states or roles to each of which is assigned specific rights and duties. Each individual can have many roles, but the roles are like the successive layers of an onion; when they are all peeled away there is nothing left. It is social institutions which define roles and one becomes a person by learning to fulfil such roles. The individual becomes a person by the grace of society and subsists only as such.

Both *prosopon* and *persona* remain highly ambiguous definitions of the personal being of the human and indicate the continuing dilemma of modern society and its social and individual neuroses. Over against this development, which drastically shapes society's tacit assumptions about the nature of the human person, the church developed its understanding of person in relation to the dogma of the Trinity. Here the idea of person is no longer understood to be an adjunct of being whose reality is defined by external factors in the form of the state, society, gods, fate. Here, far from being an adjunct to something, person comes to mean being itself.

To arrive at this unique development of thought, given the context in which the early church expressed its understanding of the faith, the church fathers undertook a Herculean task turning upside down the Greek metaphysics of the contemporary world view. Those who maintain that the early church's dogma was simply a transposition of the faith into the categories of abstract Greek metaphysics do not know either Greek metaphysics or the church's faith. The church fathers first brought together the biblical view which understands the world to be created by God out of nothing (*creatio ex nihilo*). This view traces the origin of the world to a Being who is not tied by necessity to the world but in majestic freedom relates to the world in an act of gracious condescension. By this means the fundamental premise of Greek metaphysics was denied, that is, on the basis of the way in which God has acted in the incarnation of God's Son, Jesus Christ. The closed metaphysics of the Greek idea of the God/world relationship was broken open. The existence of the world was the product of an act of freedom, of grace, of love. The being of the world and its relationship to God was freed of necessity. The world and/or God was no longer the fate of human beings.[4]

Secondly, the church fathers saw the unity of God as consisting not in an impersonal substance but in the being of

---

4.   Cf Karl Barth's insightful analysis of Western theological method along similar lines in 'Schicksal und Idee', in *Theologishe Fragen und Antworten* (Zollikon: Evangelischer Verlag, 1957).

the Father. The one God is not the one substance but the Father who generates the Son and from whom the Spirit proceeds. The unity of God is emphatically personal and relational. The personal existence of the Father constitutes God's substance in which the three persons eternally coinhere.

This of course raises the problem which is endemic in the Western doctrine of the Trinity, stemming as it does from Tertullian and Augustine, where the unity of God in terms of common substance was understood *prior to* God's three-foldness. Here person came to be defined by intra-trinitarian relationships rather than by God's action *ad extra*. The relationships between the divine persons came to be identified with the persons themselves. The relationships, instead of being unique characteristics of persons, are identified with the persons. Saint Thomas Aquinas was later to write, *persona est relatio* ('person is relation'). When the common nature assumes the first place in thinking about the Trinity the persons are obscured by an impersonal abstract essence. Consequently, in Western theology the personal relationship between God and the creature devolves into a relationship within the divine nature as such, and further expresses itself in a mysticism of impersonal spirituality centring on the individual, for example, in self-realisation, in new age thinking, or in an intellectualism devoid of personal experience.[5]

The dogma of the Trinity and creation ensured for the church that God's relationship with the world presupposed a personal relationship with the creature, realised through Christ in the Spirit with the Father. The eternal survival of the person as unique and yet related, an unrepeatably free entity loved and made free to love, constitutes the basis of the Christian view of salvation experienced in the church as new creation. Jesus Christ does not justify the title Saviour because he brings information about God. It is because he is God's personalising

---

5.   On this see K Rahner, *The Trinity* (London: Burns & Oates, 1970), 9-48.

being in relation to human beings, the one through whom created being is united to the personal being of God. The church, constituted through baptism into Christ, is the vocation of every human being; in its fellowship created personhood is fulfilled. Human life as per Woody Allen's experience of alienation and escapism from the nothingness of despair is healed, and the foundation of human community established within creation.

Consequently, the mission of the church is not to be found by determining its sociological relevance to a society which has lost the basis of personal being. As if the reality of the church was some sort of quantum which could be manipulated to fill a religious niche in the perceived need of the world. On the contrary, the mission of the church is to realise to the full its vocation of being the focus in creation of the possibility of personal being as the gift of grace, fulfilled in a community of service. The church's mission is by word and action to call all people to participate in this vocation.

Biblical References

Biblical References

8:2	148
9:22	148
14:24	120
14:61	140
16:16	112

Luke

1:15	21n
1:41	113
4:40	174
7:10	172
7:13	148, 149
10:33	148
15:20	148
19:12	118
22:19	117, 126
23:42	127

John

1:1-3	183
1:1	174
1:14	180, 188
1:29	139, 140
4:22	136
13:2	110
16:15	21n
17:19	21n, 193

Acts

4:7	90
7	6
8:32	140

Romans

3:21-25	121
6:6	98
6:8	98
6:9	205

6:10	125
8:3	141
8:17	98
8:19ff	24, 176
11:17ff	135
12:13	99
15:3	204
15:27	99

First Corinthians

1:21	172
10:16-17	119
11:2	111
11:23	111
11:26	127
12:26-27	202
15:3	111

Second Corinthians

1:18ff	121
3:18	142
4:4	141
5:17	139, 175, 176
6:11-12	148
7:3	98
7:13ff	148
8:23	98, 99
13:13	98

Galatians

2:16	121
2:20	121
3:13	141
3:22	121
3:26	139, 175
4:6	142
5:6	139, 175
6:2	204

Index

Index